"The Twisted Soul Cookbook *is a fun and funky combination of uptown, downtown, urban, country, down-home, and global recipes. Coupled with loads of bright, colorful photography, you feel the joy in this cookbook, just like you feel the joy when you meet Deborah and eat in her restaurant. Twisted Soul delivers bold yet balanced flavors, opening up a world of exciting tastes and mind-blowing combinations for cooks at any level. It's a must have on your kitchen shelf."* — VIRGINIA WILLIS, chef and James Beard Award-winning cookbook author

"We've long adored the striking originality and comforting indulgence of Deborah VanTrece's cooking. The Twisted Soul Cookbook *evolves Southern traditions with inspiration from VanTrece's own well-traveled life, mining resonances to soul she found in iconic comfort foods from Italy to France to Israel to Argentina. In VanTrece's kitchen, neck bones meet gnocchi, green tomatoes are chopped into chimichurri, and crème brûlée gets the red velvet treatment. There are so many good food ideas in this book, so beautifully executed, we can't wait for the world to devour it!"* — MATT LEE and TED LEE, authors of *The Lee Bros. Charleston Kitchen*

"The Twisted Soul Cookbook, *without any doubt, is not only about the delicious traditions of both soul & Southern food, it further establishes both as the cuisine of America—all centered around Deborah's hospitality and inclusion of all seated at the table."* — TODD RICHARDS, chef and author of *Soul: The Evolution of a Chef in 150 Recipes*

"*In her debut cookbook, Deborah VanTrece doesn't just take us around the world, she brings us home. Filled with stories and flavors,* The Twisted Soul Cookbook *reminds us that every meal we prepare is an opportunity to have some fun."* — JULIA TURSHEN, bestselling cookbook author and founder of Equity at the Table

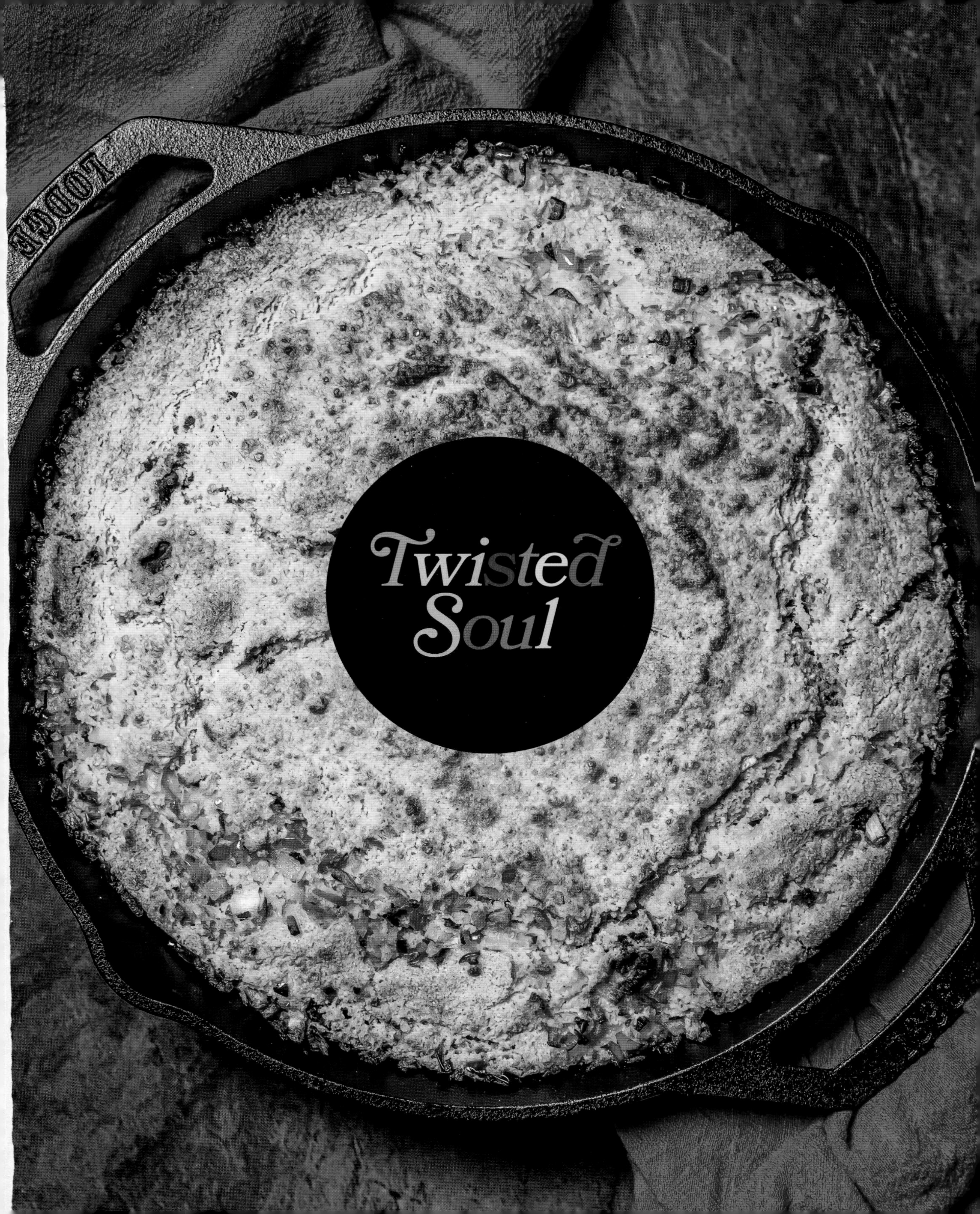
Twisted
Soul
LODGE

The Twisted Soul Cookbook

MODERN SOUL FOOD
WITH GLOBAL FLAVORS

Deborah VanTrece

WITH PHOTOGRAPHY BY

Noah Fecks

RIZZOLI
NEW YORK

New York · Paris · London · Milan

*This book is dedicated to all the women
in my life who have shaped me and given me
a strong foundation.*

The Twisted Soul Cookbook
Modern Soul Food with Global Flavors
First published in the United States of America in 2021 by
Rizzoli International Publications, Inc.
300 Park Avenue South
New York, NY 10010
rizzoliusa.com

© 2021 by Deborah VanTrece
twistedsoulcookhouseandpours.com

Photography by Noah Fecks
noahfecks.com

Publisher: Charles Miers
Editor: Jono Jarrett
Design: Janice Shay / Pinafore Press
Production Manager: Barbara Sadick
Managing Editor: Lynn Scrabis

Printed in China
2021 2022 2023 2024 / 10 9 8 7 6 5 4 3 2 1

ISBN: 9780847869695
Library of Congress Control Number: 2020941315

Visit us online:
Facebook.com/RizzoliNewYork
Twitter: @Rizzoli_Books
Instagram.com/RizzoliBooks
Pinterest.com/RizzoliBooks
Youtube.com/user/RizzoliNY

CONTENTS

INTRODUCTION

The history of soul food seems to place it in time, starting with when it became part of our food lexicon; and most people assume that it must remain static, as a sort of celebration of a time gone by. We never want to forget the importance of our basic foods and their history, but we aren't the same people our ancestors were.

I want to create new food memories—and that's what soul food does. Regional cuisines keep being redefined by time and place. Soul food means different things to different people, according to where they come from. The current food conversation is all about diversity. I grew up eating turnips, mustard greens, collards, and spinach all cooked together. In my restaurant now, I mix all these in a dish that blends the flavors and balances the textures—and I relish a twisting together of similar dishes from different cuisines, such as my Pork Neck Bones with Dill Potato Gnocchi (page 30) and Smothered Chicken Gizzard Poutine (page 31).

People of different cultures blend and mix, so it seems natural that our foods do, too. This folding in of regional and global differences to create something new, bringing old cooking techniques to life again with modern dishes, keeps a cuisine from becoming stagnant and honors the roots of soul at the same time. Those connections between soul food and the traditional comfort cooking of cuisines from around the world are easier to see than ever before.

Let me say this about soul food today: it's important to continue to build on the basic recipes in order to keep the cuisine alive. We need to create new dishes using global ingredients available locally that weren't accessible before; and we need to honor the food of African American women such as Edna Lewis and Princess Pamela and Leah Chase by returning to their recipes for inspiration. This was my goal in creating this book.

The recipes in this book represent three different takes on the soul food that I create and nurture: traditional soul dishes with my personal twist; globally inspired traditional foods (comfort foods of other countries) that I've made simple and easy for home cooks; and new soul recipes using sustainable foods with a broad range of regional and international flavors. My goal with these recipes is to give the home cook dishes that have one foot in the past, foods that taste familiar but with a distinctive difference, and are simple and easy to prepare, using mostly what you already have in your pantry.

~~~~~~~~~~~~~~~~~~~~~~~~~~~~~~~~~~

I grew up in Kansas City, Missouri, eating chitlins. I knew it back then as soul food, although the only local restaurant that served our food was called Ruby's, a little place in a Black neighborhood near 18th and Vine. A historic district now (home to the American Jazz Museum and the Negro Leagues Baseball Museum), 18th and Vine was called the Jazz district, and was famous between 1920 and 1940 for its nightlife, nightclubs, and barbecue. My momma was from that neighborhood, and the soul food I grew up knowing was what she cooked at home for us every day.

Chitlins are a pain to cook and a bigger pain to smell. The house stinks while you're cooking them, but they sure tasted good the way Momma fixed them. If you're African American, you can discuss chitlins because you know them—they're part of our food memories and everybody has a story. I was in a market in France once and saw a chitlin sausage—not called that, of course; the French call it andouillette, and it's considered a delicacy in that country. Now I serve chitlin sausage on our menu. Hog-head cheese has recently been popping up at food festivals. Neck bones, local oysters, pigs' feet—

in many cases, these cast-off cuts are already familiar in traditional African American kitchens. The fact that soul food is a cuisine based on using all these humble parts is a plus for the sustainability movement, and an important way that soul food can keep evolving from its roots.

In 1983, I left the food bubble of my Kansas City home and became a flight attendant. I moved to Dallas, where I befriended a nice guy named Ron Richey and we became roommates. His grandmother lived about five miles from our apartment and he often took me there for lunch or supper. A little old white lady, I was surprised that she was very accepting of her grandson bringing a Black girl to her perfect little house. To my surprise, she always laid a table of what I had known to be soul food: black-eyed peas, turnips, crowder peas, stewed okra, fried corn, smothered pork chops, and fried slabs of ham. I realized then that what I had been raised to believe was Black people's food had a much more diverse and complex heritage, assuring it a broader popularity. It wasn't just food from the neighborhood I grew up in. It blew me away to see this little white lady passing around the black-eyed peas, and my friend Ron gobbling them up, as he must have every day for years. To them it was just good Southern food. I was intrigued.

In 1986 I moved to Atlanta to get married. I was still a flight attendant at the time, but I always had a knack for cooking, and once I mastered the food my family liked, I scoured cookbooks to prepare new dishes I was becoming familiar with in my travels. During the next few years my former husband's job took him to France, Spain, Italy, Israel, Argentina, and Switzerland, and I went with him. In each place I ate in people's homes and learned about food traditions of other countries and cultures. I began to think that every culture has its traditional dishes that become their comfort foods, akin to the soul food I had grown up with. Spain's paella, France's duck confit and cassoulets, the hummus from Israel, the simply perfect salads in Argentina as well as their dulce de leche, and all things chocolate in Switzerland—these are some of the new tastes I experienced and fell in love with. Needless to say, I learned to cook every one of them.

The American flight attendants went on strike in 1993, and for the first time I felt vulnerable in my job. The strike didn't last long, but it helped me make a decision to change my life. I was ready for a job with less travel. I began to dream about being a caterer. I loved cooking for friends and family (often big groups!), and I was eager to share some of the international dishes I'd learned from other food cultures.

First, though, I needed the training of culinary school to take my love of cooking to the next step.

In culinary school, while I learned a great deal about French cooking techniques and "international cuisine," I soon discovered that no respect was given to African American cuisine. We spent all of one day on soul food, which for that curriculum was defined as "other." I began to think that the simplicity of soul food dishes and the use of inexpensive cuts of meat were what gave the food I loved a bad rap. (Ironically, today those sustainable and simple preparations are vitally important not only to chefs but to home cooks, too.)

I became determined to give soul food a higher profile with my cooking and catering. At the same time, Southern food was exploding in popularity all over the country. Like soul food, Southern food was mostly considered by the rest of the country to be just comfort food—simple foods, cooked in simple ways, and notoriously rich in fat. I bought Charlie Trotter's books and studied his recipes—and found oxtail recipes! I began to see how soul food and Southern food were intertwined. So many dishes were the same things I grew up eating! Of course, we now know that many Southern dishes came directly from slave cooks on plantations, handed down through both Black and white families.

Still, the soul food I knew—making a common cast-off, throwaway, disrespected food into something luxurious, tender, and tasty—stood apart from Southern food in many ways. The resounding belief in the Black community was if the food looked good, it couldn't taste good. I became motivated to think about how I could apply the techniques I had learned in culinary school to my food heritage. I knew soul food could both look good and taste good. The many soul food restaurants in Atlanta offered good food and great service, but they were more like diners or cafeterias, not at all a fine dining experience. I was thrilled when Sylvia's from Harlem opened a beautifully decorated, refined, white tablecloth soul food restaurant in Atlanta.

A turning point for me as a chef was serving food to the consulates during the 1996 Olympic games in Atlanta. I was tasked to create recipes celebrating the foods of different countries, a chance for me to pull upon my experiences eating in real homes around the world. All my food memories of those traditional dishes came back to me, and I was able to bring authenticity to the food I made because I had enjoyed and experimented with those flavors before. This pointed me toward a broader definition of soul food.

Not long after, in 1998, I was planning my first restaurant menu when I had an aha moment. I had the idea of making a stuffed grape leaf, one of my favorite Greek recipes, using the most basic soul dish—collard greens—as the wrapping. Tradition was you cooked greens down, sometimes you added turnips or meat, but these leaves weren't widely used for any other soul dishes. My collard roll was a success, and it inspired me to try other ways to reinterpret and reapply food principles. Now I serve collard green slaw, collard pesto, collard Caesar salad, collard green chimichurri, pickled collard greens—well, you get the idea. Soul food has evolved and I want to share it with you in this cookbook.

I don't look for the differences in food anymore, I look for commonalities, similarities, and how to combine flavors. Anyone who tells me a story about a dish that reminds them of what their grandmother used to cook, I try to figure out how to make it, and inevitably what to add and how to build on the dish. The more I learn, the more I'm able to create layered dishes that are soul-satisfying enough to create new memories.

I work to bring soul food into our 21st-century's flavor-forward culture. Let this book be a catalyst for you, the home cook, to create your own food memories. Try these simple, inexpensive recipes. Try the sauces you like on other meats you cook. Pair the sides with your own favorite dishes. Have a dinner party and impress your friends with something different, yet somehow similar to what they know and love. It's not just soul food because of its historic roots in African American culture, but because it comes from the soul and feeds the soul, whether your grandmother cooked grape leaves or collard greens.

Now, go cook!

Castoffs and Throwaways

Port-Braised Oxtails

Oxtail Rillettes

Braised Turkey Necks

Candied Salmon Belly Bacon

Spicy Pig Ear Salad

Smoked Chicken Cracklin' Cornbread

Slow-Cooked Beef Tongue Pot Roast
with Wild Mushroom Gravy

Braised Chitterlings
with Spicy Apple and Onion Gastrique

Mr. Albert's Hog-Head Cheese

Bologna Mousse

Beef Cheek and Goat Cheese Lasagna

Pork Neck Bones with Dill Potato Gnocchi

Smothered Chicken Gizzard Poutine

Deep-Fried Fish Bone Brittle

PORT-BRAISED OXTAILS

SERVES 6

5 pounds oxtails, trimmed of
   excess fat
1 tablespoon kosher salt
1 tablespoon freshly cracked
   black pepper
2 teaspoons garlic powder
2 teaspoons onion powder
½ teaspoon ground cloves
½ teaspoon ground ginger
2 cups all-purpose flour, divided
¾ cup vegetable oil
6 cups beef broth
2 cups port
½ cup cognac
2 medium carrots, coarsely
   chopped
2 celery stalks, coarsely chopped
1 large onion, coarsely chopped
4 cloves garlic, smashed

Oxtails are exactly what they sound like. The oxtail is packed with rich, flavorful marrow. Surprisingly, oxtail recipes are found pretty much worldwide, including from China, Spain, Jamaica, and Ghana. For years, oxtail was ignored in this country by most chefs and home cooks outside the African American communities, but now it's available pre-cut in segments in almost any market or grocery, and has found its way onto many tables.

I've updated this recipe with the additions of port, cognac, clove, and ginger, which add a hint of sweetness to the richness of the meat. These layers of aromatic flavors allow the meat to pair with a wider array of different starches or vegetables.

Rinse the oxtails, pat them dry, and place in a large bowl.

In a small bowl, stir together the salt, pepper, garlic powder, onion powder, cloves, and ginger. Rub this seasoning all over the oxtails and place them on a sheet pan or a piece of parchment.

Using the same large bowl, toss the oxtails in ¾ cup flour, to coat.

In a Dutch oven or large high-sided skillet, heat the vegetable oil over medium. When the oil is hot, add the oxtails, taking care not to crowd the pan (work in batches if necessary), and brown them for 5 to 6 minutes on each side, using tongs to turn the meat, until the oxtails are well browned. Transfer to a large roasting pan, reserving the cooking oil in the Dutch oven, and set aside while you make the gravy.

Preheat the oven to 350 degrees F.

To make the gravy, let the oil cool for 10 minutes, then pour it through a fine-mesh sieve into a bowl or small pan to remove dark particles. Return the strained oil to the same Dutch oven or large skillet.

Over medium heat, whisk in the remaining 1¼ cups flour a small amount at a time, and cook, whisking, until the flour turns a caramel brown. Whisking continuously, slowly stream in the beef broth, then the port and cognac. Continue to whisk until the gravy is smooth and free of lumps. Reduce the heat to medium-low and simmer for 20 minutes, then stir in 2 cups water, the carrots, celery, onion, and garlic. Simmer for 10 more minutes and taste. Add additional salt and pepper as needed.

Pour the gravy over the oxtails in the roasting pan, adding water as needed to fully cover. Cover the pan, transfer to the oven, and cook for 4 hours, or until the meat is falling-off-the-bone tender.

Serve over rice, noodles, potatoes, barley, or Boursin Cheese Grits (page 88). Don't waste any leftover gravy. Or refrigerate in a lidded container for up to 7 days, and warm over low heat with the addition of a little water to loosen the gravy before serving.

OXTAIL RILLETTES

MAKES 3 TO 3 ½ CUPS

4 to 5 pounds Port-Braised Oxtails (page 13), removed from gravy, at room temperature

8 tablespoons (1 stick) unsalted butter, divided

2 shallots, chopped

2 teaspoons grated orange peel

2 tablespoons cognac

2 teaspoons whole green peppercorns, drained

1 teaspoon finely chopped fresh thyme

¼ teaspoon ground allspice

½ cup reserved gravy from Port-Braised Oxtails (page 13)

Kosher salt

The rich, beef flavor and dense, spreadable texture of these rillettes come from the luxurious use of braised oxtails and their gravy. Rillettes are indispensable around the holidays when unexpected guests drop by; they are a great way to use any leftover oxtails. You can use any size crock or mold, and the rillettes will keep for a week in the refrigerator—so they are perfect to make ahead or for impromptu entertaining. On its own, this recipe makes a decadent hors d'oeuvre or starter with an aperitif, but also shines as part of an impressive charcuterie platter. This is a dish that can go from humble to fancy depending upon the occasion.

Using your hands, or two forks, pull the meat from the oxtails, discarding the fat and bones. Transfer the meat to a food processor.

In a small pan over medium heat, melt 3 tablespoons butter, add the shallots, and sauté for 5 to 7 minutes, until the shallots begin to caramelize.

Add the remaining 5 tablespoons butter, the orange zest, cognac, green peppercorns, thyme, allspice, reserved gravy, and cooked shallots to the food processor with the shredded oxtails, and pulse until the mixture is finely minced, but not completely smooth, about 8 to 10 pulses. You want to leave some texture to the meat.

Transfer the mixture to a bowl, taste, and add salt as needed. Press into a crock or mold, cover with plastic wrap, and refrigerate at least 2 hours before serving.

Serve the rillettes at room temperature or warmed in a 200-degree F oven for 10 minutes, with crusty bread, Avocado Hoecakes (page 198), or crackers.

BRAISED TURKEY NECKS

SERVES 8

5 pounds turkey necks (about 8)
1 tablespoon kosher salt
1 tablespoon freshly cracked
  black pepper
2 teaspoons herbes de Provence
1 teaspoon garlic powder
1 teaspoon onion powder
¼ cup vegetable oil
2 medium yellow onions, finely
  chopped
2 shallots, minced
4 cloves garlic, minced
4 stalks celery, chopped
2 bay leaves
¼ cup all-purpose flour
3 cups chicken broth
1 cup dry red wine

As a kid growing up I learned that my family had an affinity for bones with meat on them, not meat with bones. My grandmother would claim that sometimes this was all that she could afford, and she learned early on that a small amount of meat with a lot of bone could produce meals that were wholesome and very flavorful. Fish collars, beef and pork neck bones, and fried fish bones (page 32) are a few examples.

I have tweaked my grandmother's recipe for braised turkey necks with the addition of dry red wine and herbes de Provence, to give this dish even more depth of flavor. I especially like to serve it over Boursin Cheese Grits (page 88), which my grandmother would never have imagined but I think would really enjoy. I like to use both onions and shallots because they each add a different flavor to the dish.

Rinse the turkey necks under cold running water for 2 minutes, pulling off and discarding any bits of fat. Blot with a paper towel to remove excess water. Place in a large bowl and set aside.

In a small bowl, stir together the salt, pepper, herbes de Provence, garlic powder, and onion powder. Sprinkle thoroughly over the turkey necks and toss well to season.

Heat the vegetable oil in a large skillet over medium-high heat. Carefully add the turkey necks, and sear for about 5 minutes on each side, until the necks are well browned.

Transfer the browned turkey necks to a Dutch oven, leaving the oil in the skillet. Cover the turkey necks with the onions, shallots, garlic, celery, and bay leaves.

Preheat the oven to 350 degrees F.

Put the skillet with the drippings back over medium heat, and quickly whisk in the flour to make a roux. Stir constantly for 8 minutes, or until it turns light brown, then slowly whisk in the chicken broth and wine until no lumps remain. Reduce the heat to low and simmer for 15 minutes, or until thickened.

Pour the gravy over the vegetables and turkey necks in the Dutch oven. Cover and bake until the necks are tender, about 3 hours.

Remove from the oven and let cool for 20 minutes. Serve over rice, potatoes, or grits.

CANDIED SALMON BELLY BACON

SERVES 12

3 cups packed dark brown sugar
2½ cups kosher salt
3 pounds salmon belly, skin removed, cut in thin strips
½ cup maple syrup

My local fish market has a section labeled "cheap." I shop there for two reasons: One, because I like deals(!); and two, it's full of parts that yield impressive, flavorful dishes, but are usually bypassed in favor of prettier, easier-cooking cuts. Among the offerings are shells, bones, fish heads, and lots of trimmed pieces left over from cutting more costly fillets. When lucky, I find salmon belly. Sure, they are sometimes fatty, but the belly holds high levels of omega-3 fatty acids, so it's good fat. Fish markets that butcher their own salmon usually have this lying around and are willing to give it up fairly cheap.

This recipe is attributed to Pacific Northwest Native American tribes who would cure salmon belly in anticipation of long winters. I decided to tweak it as a great alternative to traditional pork bacon for breakfast or brunch, because it covers similar flavor profiles but with better fat. Try it served with eggs, or used in eggs Benedict.

You will need an outdoor grill with a hood or a stovetop smoker and hickory wood chunks to smoke the salmon belly. This technique is easy but takes several days to do correctly. Salmon belly is often sold in irregular pieces according to how the fishmonger has cut it. For this recipe, I used 8-inch-long pieces, similar to sliced bacon. Simply trim your pieces as desired.

To make the cure, mix the sugar and salt together in a bowl. In a large casserole dish or large lidded container, lay down a thin layer of the sugar-salt mixture. Next, place a single layer of salmon belly strips on top of the mixture, arranging them as close as possible with no overlap. Top the salmon belly with another layer of the sugar-salt mixture, packing it tightly with your hands. Repeat until all of the salmon is well covered by the sugar-salt mixture.

Cover the dish tightly and refrigerate for 1 to 2 hours at the most. The longer salmon belly sits in the cure the saltier it will become.

Remove the salmon belly from the pan and rinse each piece under cool running water, pat them dry with a paper towel, and lay flat in a single layer on a tray or sheet pan. Refrigerate uncovered for 12 to 24 hours, until the salmon belly has dried and is slightly hardened, similar to crisp bacon.

Remove the grate from your grill or smoker, and prepare the grill for indirect cooking by placing a small amount of charcoal and starter on one side of the smoker. Light the coals.

In a medium bowl, soak 2 cups wood chips in water. Once the smoker has reached 225 to 250 degrees F, and the charcoal has turned white, place one-fourth of the wood chips directly on the charcoal.

Spray the grate with nonstick cooking spray and set into the smoker. Carefully place the salmon belly strips on the cool side of the grill (not directly over the coals). Brush each strip generously with maple syrup. Close the lid and smoke over low heat for 1½ to 2 hours, basting the salmon belly every 30 minutes with maple syrup until it's firm to the touch and lacquered glossy-brown in color.

Transfer to a clean sheet pan, baste again with maple syrup, and let cool slightly before serving.

The glazed salmon belly can be stored, layered, in a sealed container or a resealable plastic bag, and refrigerated for up to 2 weeks. It also freezes well. To reheat, brush it with a little maple syrup and warm it in a preheated 325-degree F oven for 5 to 7 minutes.

SPICY PIG EAR SALAD

SERVES 8

PIG EARS

2 to 2½ pounds pig ears (about 4 large)
1 cup dry white wine
1 medium yellow onion, coarsely chopped
5 cloves garlic, smashed
3 bay leaves
2 tablespoons kosher salt
2 tablespoons ground cumin
1 tablespoon granulated garlic
1 tablespoon granulated onion
½ teaspoon cayenne pepper
1 cup cornstarch
Vegetable oil, for frying

SALAD

5 Roma tomatoes, diced
1 cup shredded carrots
1 red pepper, thinly sliced
2 stalks celery, thinly sliced
6 scallions, chopped
1 large head romaine lettuce, trimmed and torn

DRESSING

2 jalapeños, seeded and diced
Juice of 3 limes (about ½ cup)
2 tablespoons agave syrup
1 cup chopped cilantro leaves
1 teaspoon kosher salt
¼ cup red wine vinegar
⅓ cup olive oil

While traveling through Mexico City, I came across a small authentic restaurant that offered this amazing dish as a starter. The addition of pig ears to salad ingredients was something new to my palate—I certainly never saw that in the soul food of my youth—but the classic preparation of the pig ears was almost the same as my grandmother's method. I have used this dish as an unexpected addition to my frequent home barbecues. I love dishes that evoke conversation and this one definitely does the trick.

Soul food is about spicing and seasoning, so the way to make cuts taste good is to add extra flavor. That's why I sometimes use both granulated and fresh garlic and onions in dishes like this one. Note that pig ears come in all sizes. Wherever you buy them, the butcher or grocer will weigh them for you.

MAKE THE PIG EARS: Using a lighter, burn any visible hair off the skin. Rinse the ears thoroughly under cold running water, place them in a large Dutch oven or heavy-bottomed pot, and cover with cold water. Bring to a boil over high heat and boil for about 15 minutes. Drain, then refill the pot with just enough water to cover the ears. Add the wine, onion, garlic, bay leaves, salt, cumin, granulated garlic, granulated onion, and cayenne pepper. Cover the pot and cook over medium heat for 3 hours, or until the pig ears are fork tender. Replenish the water as needed during cooking.

Remove the ears from the pot with a slotted spoon and transfer to a sheet pan to cool. Cover with foil and refrigerate for at least 2 hours. Once chilled, cut the pig ears into ¼-inch-thick strips. Sprinkle with cornstarch and toss to coat.

In a large skillet, heat 1 inch of vegetable oil over medium-high heat until it registers 350 degrees F on a deep-fry thermometer. Shake any excess cornstarch from the pig ears and fry in batches, being careful not to overcrowd the skillet. Cook for 4 to 5 minutes, until the ear strips turn slightly brown and get crispy, turning as needed to keep them from sticking together. Remove with a slotted spoon to a paper-towel-lined bowl to drain. Repeat until all strips have been browned. Let the ears cool to room temperature.

MAKE THE SALAD: In a large bowl, toss the tomatoes, carrots, peppers, celery, scallions, and romaine lettuce. Top with the pig ears.

MAKE THE DRESSING: In a blender, combine the jalapeños, lime juice, agave, cilantro, salt, and vinegar and blend until the ingredients are well-mixed but still retain some texture. Slowly drizzle in the olive oil with the motor on. Pour half the dressing over the salad, and reserve the remainder to pass around the table. The dressing can be made a day ahead and refrigerated until ready to use. It will keep, refrigerated, in a covered container for 7 to 10 days.

To serve, arrange some vegetable salad on a plate, top with a portion of the fried pig ears, and sprinkle with a small amount of the reserved dressing.

SMOKED CHICKEN
CRACKLIN' CORNBREAD

SERVES 8

Skin from 3 to 5 pounds uncooked chicken (about 16 pieces)
¼ teaspoon smoked paprika
½ teaspoon kosher salt
¼ teaspoon garlic powder
¼ teaspoon onion powder
¼ cup lard (or shortening or unsalted butter)
½ cup finely diced red peppers
½ cup finely diced onion
1 jalapeño, finely diced
2 cups self-rising cornmeal
½ cup all-purpose flour
3 tablespoons packed brown sugar
2 large eggs, lightly beaten
2½ cups buttermilk

Coming from humble beginnings, you learn not to throw anything way. Cracklin' cornbread is a traditional soul food. I've tweaked this popular dish to feature another tasty castoff, taking some inspiration from schmaltz and gribenes, which is a classic Jewish dish of crispy chicken skin with onions. Although I love recipes that call for skinless pieces of chicken, I am also very respectful of the awesome flavor that comes from chicken skin. I buy whole chickens and break them down myself, freezing the skin of any pieces that I prefer to serve skinless. This often includes breast, thighs, and backs, and after accumulating a decent amount of skins, I like to make chicken cracklin' as a snack (akin to pork rinds), or crumbled on a salad, or added to scrambled eggs.

You will need an outdoor grill with a hood or a stovetop smoker and wood chips for this recipe.

Use your hands to remove the skin from the chicken pieces. Rinse the skin and place on a paper-towel-lined platter. Pat dry to remove excess water from the skin.

In a small bowl, stir together the paprika, kosher salt, garlic powder, and onion powder. Sprinkle this seasoning over both sides of the chicken skin.

Remove the grate from your grill or smoker, and prepare it for indirect cooking by placing a small amount of charcoal and starter on one side of the smoker. Light the coals.

In a medium bowl, soak ¼ cup wood chips in water. Once the smoker has reached 225 to 250 degrees F, and the charcoal has turned white, place the wood chips directly on the charcoal. Spray the grate with nonstick cooking spray and replace on the grill.

Carefully place the chicken skin on the grate on the indirect heat side of the smoker. Cover and smoke for 15 to 20 minutes, until the chicken skin begins to darken.

Preheat the oven to 325 degrees F.

Transfer the smoked skin to parchment-paper-lined sheet pans, laying the skin flat. Cover with another sheet pan and press down to further flatten the skin. Put the pans in the oven and roast the skins for 10 minutes, then use tongs to flip the skins, cover again with the sheet pan, and roast for another 12 to 15 minutes, until they are crispy.

Remove from the oven and pour off excess chicken fat into a small container (it will probably be a few tablespoons) for use in the cornbread later. Once the chicken cracklin' has cooled, break it into ½-inch pieces and set aside.

Increase the oven heat to 400 degrees F.

Place the reserved chicken fat, lard, red peppers, onion, and jalapeño in a 10-inch cast-iron skillet, and put the skillet in the oven to warm while mixing the remaining ingredients.

In a large bowl whisk together the cornmeal, flour, sugar, and eggs. Add the buttermilk and stir just until combined. Gently fold in the reserved cracklin'. Remove the cast-iron skillet from the oven and pour the cornbread batter into the hot pan on top of the fat and vegetables. Do not stir. Return the skillet to the oven and bake for 25 to 30 minutes, until golden brown and firm to the touch.

Cool slightly before cutting, and serve with your favorite beans, soup, or Brunswick Stew (page 66).

SLOW-COOKED BEEF TONGUE POT ROAST *With Wild Mushroom Gravy*

SERVES 8 TO 10

3 tablespoons vegetable oil

2 medium yellow onions, quartered

4 carrots, sliced lengthwise

1 fennel bulb, sliced

6 cloves garlic, smashed

2 (3-pound) beef tongues

6 cups beef broth

2 tablespoons whole black peppercorns

2 teaspoons Lawry's Seasoned Salt

2 teaspoons kosher salt

3 bay leaves

4 sprigs fresh thyme

2 teaspoons prepared horseradish

1 teaspoon dry mustard

12 ounces wild mushrooms (shiitake, cremini, or chanterelles are my favorites), cleaned, stemmed, and cut in half

4 tablespoons cornstarch

One of the great things about true comfort food is you can serve the same dish in different ways and enjoy it just as much each time. You can prepare this pot roast early in the week and enjoy leftovers over the next few days—served hot with creamy mashed potatoes, as a great chopped sandwich filling, or sliced and served cold with raw onions, horseradish, and mustard.

This dish has more flavor and is prettier than the typical boiled beef tongue.

Heat the oil in a large Dutch oven or heavy-bottomed pot over medium heat. Add the onions, carrots, fennel, and garlic and sweat for about 5 minutes, then remove from the pot and set aside.

Add the beef tongues, broth, peppercorns, seasoned salt, salt, bay leaves, thyme, horseradish, and dry mustard, and bring to a simmer.

Add enough water to cover the tongues with 3 inches of liquid. Add the onion and carrot mixture, cover the pot, and continue to cook over medium-low heat for 4 hours. Remove the lid, add the mushrooms, and taste for seasoning. Cover and cook for another 2 hours. The tongue is done when you can pierce it easily with a paring knife with little resistance. Remove the Dutch oven from the heat. Using tongs, remove the tongues and transfer them to a cutting board to cool for 20 minutes.

Meanwhile, make a slurry to thicken the gravy: place the cornstarch in a small bowl, and stir in 4 tablespoons cold water till smooth. Remove the thyme sprigs from the Dutch oven. Stir the slurry into the vegetables and gravy. Return the pot to medium heat for 5 to 7 minutes to heat through.

Once the tongues have cooled, use your fingers to peel off the outer skin. Trim away any excess fat, and slice the meat crosswise into thin slices. Arrange the slices on a serving platter and top with the gravy and vegetables. Serve with mashed potatoes or Collard Green Dumplings (page 86).

BRAISED CHITTERLINGS
With Spicy Apple and Onion Gastrique

SERVES 4 TO 6

10 pounds cleaned chitterlings
   (see headnote)
½ cup apple cider vinegar
10 cloves garlic, smashed
2 celery stalks, each cut
   crosswise into 4 pieces
1 large onion, coarsely chopped
1 green pepper, seeded and
   coarsely chopped
1 jalapeño, seeded and coarsely
   chopped
1 teaspoon kosher salt, plus
   more as needed
2 tablespoons Lawry's Seasoned
   Salt
2 tablespoons granulated garlic
2 tablespoons granulated onion

It's true that chitterlings are a lot of work to prepare, but if you are a connoisseur, you know they are well worth the effort. Remember that they are intestines; so, cleaning them properly is key. My mother and dad taught me how to clean chitterlings—you must have a keen eye when removing the fat and particles. To save yourself this effort, I strongly suggest purchasing a good pre-cleaned brand such as Aunt Bessie's. Trust me, it's definitely worth the extra money.

Chitterlings, probably more so than any other dish in this book, truly represent making something good out of nothing. You can find chitterlings used in sausages in France, cooked with oregano and spices in Turkey, and fried and served with fries in Spain. In this recipe, I pair the chitterlings with a gastrique, which is a sweet and tart condiment found in French cuisine. The acid provided by the vinegar cuts through the fat and adds a perfect balance to the meal.

This rich, hearty dish is labor-intensive, so it's typically saved for the Thanksgiving, Christmas, or New Year's Day table in Black communities. I love it anytime with coleslaw and cornbread!

In a large lidded pot, combine the chitterlings, vinegar, and enough water to cover. Bring just to a boil over medium-high heat, then strain into a colander, discarding the water. Rinse out the pot.

Return the chitterlings to the clean pot and once again add water to cover. Add the garlic, celery, onion, green pepper, jalapeño, salt, seasoned salt, granulated garlic, and granulated onion. Bring to a boil over medium-high heat, cover, and reduce the heat to medium. Cook for 3½ to 4 hours, stirring occasionally to prevent sticking, and adding water as needed to cover the chitterlings as they cook down. The chitterlings are ready when they are tender enough to cut with a fork. Remove from the heat.

Use a slotted spoon to transfer the chitterlings to a shallow pan, and when cool enough to handle, cut them into small pieces. Taste the broth and add additional salt as needed. Return the chitterling pieces to the broth, let cool, and refrigerate overnight.

When you are ready to serve, skim the fat off the top of the chitterlings and reheat over medium heat. Serve with the gravy over rice, alongside coleslaw and Smoked Chicken Cracklin' Cornbread (page 22).

MR. ALBERT'S HOG-HEAD CHEESE

MAKES 4 MEDIUM LOAVES (ABOUT 1½ POUNDS EACH)

1 pig's head (about 10 pounds),
  split in half, brains and eyes
  removed (see headnote)
4 pigs' feet
16 cloves garlic, smashed
3 celery stalks, each cut
  crosswise into 4 pieces
3 yellow onions, quartered
6 tablespoons kosher salt
2 jalapeños, seeded and chopped
12 sprigs fresh thyme
4 bay leaves
1 cup apple cider vinegar
1 tablespoon red pepper flakes
1 cup chopped flat-leaf parsley
  leaves
Salt and freshly cracked black
  pepper
Pickled Mustard Seeds
  (page 183), for serving

Headcheese, or souse meat as it is sometimes called, is a cold cut that originated in Europe, where it was often thought of as peasant food. As chefs worldwide commit to more sustainable practices and whole animal usage, you can find some traditions for hog-head cheese reemerging in Asia, Australia, Canada, and South America. It can even be found in gourmet stores—ironically, for a pretty penny.

My memories of this dish come from my grandfather, Mr. Albert, who would make it for our family and our neighbors in the fall to last through the winter or give it away as holiday gifts. Heads are usually available from your butcher or at Asian markets, and can be fairly inexpensive. Ask your butcher to split the head in half for you and remove the brains and eyes. It's a major step you don't want to deal with yourself.

This recipe can yield quite a few loaves, depending on what size mold you use, but the headcheese freezes beautifully. Serve this dish as part of your charcuterie board, with a selection of cheeses, crackers, and Pickled Mustard Seeds.

In a large stockpot, cover the pig's head and feet with 4 inches of water, and add the garlic, celery, onions, salt, jalapeõs, thyme, and bay leaves. Bring to a rapid boil over high heat. Once the water comes to a boil, reduce the heat to medium-low and cook at a brisk simmer for 4 to 4½ hours, until the meat is falling-off-the-bone tender. As the meat cooks, use a ladle or skimmer to skim any froth off the top and discard. Once tender, use a kitchen spider or large strainer to transfer the meat to a shallow pan to cool. Set the stockpot aside to allow the broth to cool.

Strain the cooled broth and discard the solids. Combine 8 cups strained broth and the apple cider vinegar in a medium saucepan. Bring to a rapid simmer over medium-high heat and cook for 30 to 45 minutes, until the broth reduces by half to about 4 cups.

While the broth is reducing, carefully pull the meat and skin from the bones and cut it into ¾-inch pieces; discard the bones. Stir the red pepper flakes and chopped parsley into the meat, season with salt and pepper, and set aside.

Once the broth has reduced to 4 cups, stir in the meat mixture. Fill 4 medium loaf pans with the mixture, cover, and refrigerate for at least 6 hours or overnight for the loaves to set.

To serve, run a knife around the edges of the pan to loosen. Invert onto a plate and the loaf should come out cleanly. If not, warm the loaf pan by briefly submerging it halfway into a pan of hot water till the headcheese loosens. Serve with pickled mustard seeds and crackers. Leftovers can be frozen for up to 6 months, or refrigerated for 10 to 14 days.

BOLOGNA MOUSSE

MAKES ABOUT 3 CUPS (20 TO 24 OUNCES)

1 pound beef bologna, cut into
    ½-inch cubes
½ pound Italian mortadella, cut
    into ½-inch cubes
¾ cup ricotta cheese (6 ounces)
½ cup grated Parmesan cheese
¼ cup heavy cream
¼ cup chopped scallions
2 baguettes or bread of choice,
    sliced, for serving
Pickled Mustard Seeds (page
    183), for serving

As a child growing up, one of my favorite after-school snacks was a bologna and mustard sandwich on white bread. As an adult I still have an affinity for these flavors, and this recipe gives me a more refined way of enjoying them. It is a great starter to a soulful meal and always becomes a topic of conversation around food memories. This is a killer addition to any charcuterie platter alongside Pickled Mustard Seeds.

In a food processor, process the bologna and mortadella until it becomes a paste, 1 to 2 minutes. Add the remaining ingredients and process for 2 to 3 minutes longer, until the texture is thick and airy, like a mousse. Transfer the mixture to a covered container and refrigerate for at least 2 hours.

To serve, remove from the refrigerator and let sit at room temperature for 15 minutes. Spread on slices of baguette or your bread of choice and top with pickled mustard seeds. Leftover mousse will keep, refrigerated, for 7 to 10 days.

BEEF CHEEK AND GOAT CHEESE LASAGNA

SERVES 12

3 pounds beef cheeks
1 tablespoon plus 2 teaspoons
  kosher salt, divided
1 tablespoon garlic powder
1 tablespoon onion powder
2 teaspoons freshly cracked
  black pepper
½ cup extra-virgin olive oil
1 cup coarsely chopped onion
1 shallot, coarsely chopped
4 cloves garlic, smashed
1 cup coarsely chopped celery
1 cup coarsely chopped carrot
2 cups red wine
2 cups beef broth
2 teaspoons finely chopped
  fresh basil
2 teaspoons finely chopped
  fresh oregano
2 teaspoons finely chopped
  fresh thyme
3 bay leaves
1 tablespoon sugar
1 (6-ounce) can tomato paste
1 (28-ounce) can whole San
  Marzano tomatoes
16 ounces ricotta cheese
2 cups grated Parmesan cheese
2 large eggs
1 (16-ounce) box no-bake
  lasagna noodles
2 cups (16 ounces) crumbled
  goat cheese, divided into 3
  portions
2 cups shredded mozzarella
  cheese, divided into 3 portions

An inexpensive and soulful alternative to a classic Italian dish, this lasagna is a perfect way to utilize an underused cut of beef. Beef cheeks are a very tough cut that you can get from your local butcher. Braising is the best way to prepare beef cheeks, because the meat absorbs all the flavors in the pot and becomes luxuriously moist and tender. If you can't find beef cheeks, you can simply substitute beef short ribs, and remove the bones after cooking.

Make this dish several days ahead and pop it in the oven when you're ready to serve. It can be frozen prior to cooking, or leftovers can be kept frozen up to 3 months.

Trim and discard any excess fat and membranes from the beef cheeks.

In a small bowl, mix together 1 tablespoon salt, the garlic powder, onion powder, and black pepper. Rub this all over the beef cheeks.

Heat the olive oil in a Dutch oven or large heavy-bottomed pot over medium-high heat. Place the beef cheeks, a few at a time, into the pot and brown on all sides. Transfer to a plate and repeat until all the beef cheeks have been browned. Reduce the heat to medium, return the beef cheeks to the Dutch oven, and add the onions, shallot, and garlic. Sauté for 3 to 5 minutes, stirring often, until the onion is translucent. Add the celery and carrots and sauté until softened, about 3 minutes. Pour the wine into the pot and stir, scraping the brown bits from the bottom of the pan. Stir in the beef broth, basil, oregano, thyme, bay leaves, sugar, remaining 2 teaspoons salt, the tomato paste, and tomatoes. Reduce the heat to low, cover, and simmer for 2 to 2½ hours, stirring often to prevent sticking. The beef cheeks are done when they easily pull apart with a fork. Remove the pot from the heat and let cool. Use two forks to

shred the beef into the sauce.

Preheat the oven to 375 degrees F.

In a medium bowl, mix together the ricotta, Parmesan, and eggs. Ladle 1½ cups meat sauce into a lasagna pan or 13 x 9-inch baking dish. Place a layer of noodles on top of the sauce, breaking the noodles as needed to make them fit in the pan. Top with one-third of the ricotta mixture, sprinkle with one-third of the goat cheese, and top with one-third of the shredded mozzarella. Top this cheese layer with another 1½ cups meat sauce, and repeat the process to make three layers, ending with the cheese.

Cover loosely with aluminum foil and bake for 30 to 40 minutes, until the cheese bubbles around the edges and is crusty. Remove the foil and let the lasagna rest for 20 to 25 minutes before serving.

PORK NECK BONES
With Dill Potato Gnocchi

SERVES 8

6 pounds pork neck bones
2 tablespoons Lawry's Seasoned
  Salt
1 tablespoon onion powder
1 tablespoon garlic powder
1 tablespoon freshly cracked
  black pepper
1 cup coarsely chopped onion
4 cloves garlic, smashed
2 pounds large baking potatoes
  (about 4)
2 large egg yolks
1 teaspoon kosher salt
½ teaspoon ground white pepper
1 teaspoon chopped fresh dill
1½ cups all-purpose flour, plus
  more for dusting
4 tablespoons unsalted butter

Pork neck bones, very common in traditional soul cooking, are one of those things you've probably ignored in your own grocery store, but chances are they're there. They may not sound appetizing, but this dish is easy to prepare and absolutely delicious. There's a little meat and a lot of bone, but they are tender and flavorful—you can actually suck the meat off the bone! Neck bones contribute body and flavor to a broth, and can be smoked and used to flavor vegetables like greens, cabbage, or green beans, or served as a protein alongside rice or potatoes. I have paired them here with an Italian gnocchi flavored with dill—a perfect accompaniment to the rich flavors of the braised neck bones. The gnocchi drink up the delicious braising liquid and replace the usual potato element, making this a lighter version of the classic soul food dish. Uncooked gnocchi can be assembled in advance, placed on a baking sheet in one layer, covered tightly, and frozen until ready for use, or up to 2 months.

Rinse the neck bones under cold running water. Trim off any excess fat, veins, and thick cartilage. In a large pot, combine the neck bones with the seasoning salt, onion powder, garlic powder, black pepper, onions, and garlic cloves with enough water to cover. Set over medium-high heat and cook for 15 to 20 minutes, until the liquid comes to a boil. Reduce the heat to medium, cover, and cook for 2 to 2½ hours, stirring occasionally. The neck bones are done when the bones pull apart easily.

Remove the neck bones from the broth and set aside. Continue to reduce the broth over medium heat for 30 to 40 minutes. While the broth is simmering, prepare the gnocchi, as described below. Once the broth thickens slightly, but isn't as thick as a gravy, return the neck bones to the broth, cover, and set aside off the heat.

To make the gnocchi, place the potatoes in a large pot with enough cold water to cover them by 3 inches, and cook over medium-high heat for 10 minutes, then cover the pot with a lid and cook for 15 to 20 more minutes, until a knife easily slices through a potato.

Drain the potatoes and let them cool slightly for ease in handling. Peel and quarter them, then push them through a potato ricer into a medium bowl. Stir in the egg yolks, salt, white pepper, and dill. Add the flour and stir until a stiff dough forms. Knead the dough gently until smooth and slightly sticky.

Line a sheet pan with wax paper and dust it with flour.

On a lightly floured surface, divide the dough into 4 equal pieces and roll each piece into a long, ½- to ¾-inch-thick rope. Cut the ropes into ¾- to 1-inch lengths. Place the gnocchi dough onto the floured sheet pan, sprinkle with a little flour, and set aside.

In a large high-sided skillet over medium-high heat, bring 3 inches of salted water to a boil. Place the gnocchi in the water and cook until they float to the surface.

In another skillet over high heat, melt the butter. Using a slotted spoon, transfer the gnocchi from the boiling water to the butter and cook for 1 minute, stirring gently with a wooden spoon, to coat the gnocchi with butter. It's fine if the butter begins to brown slightly.

Distribute the gnocchi among individual serving bowls, place a few neck bones in each bowl, and ladle the broth on top.

SMOTHERED CHICKEN GIZZARD POUTINE

SERVES 8

2 pounds chicken gizzards
1½ cups buttermilk
1 teaspoon kosher salt
2 tablespoons garlic powder
2 tablespoons onion powder
1 tablespoons Lawry's Seasoned Salt
1 teaspoon paprika
½ teaspoon cayenne pepper
8 large russet potatoes, skin on
1 cup all-purpose flour
Vegetable oil, for frying
1 cup medium-diced yellow onion
2 cloves garlic, smashed
½ cup shredded carrots
½ cup coarsely chopped celery
3 cups chicken broth
1 tablespoon Worcestershire sauce
2 bay leaves
Salt and freshly ground black pepper
2 cups cheese curds, available at some grocers, farmers markets, or online
Thinly sliced scallions (optional)

This recipe is a play on a traditional poutine—the popular Canadian dish of French fries, cheese curds, and brown gravy. Who knew the Canadians had truly world-class comfort food? To make it more soulful, I added chicken gizzards, which are easily available and very inexpensive. Gizzards are a tasty protein and naturally low in fat. Although gizzards are often thrown away here, they are considered a delicacy in many cultures, such as in South Africa, where they are reserved only for the head of household.

The gravy can be made one or two days in advance then warmed up when the poutine is ready to serve. This is a perfect dish for large groups to share and a fun one to bring for tailgating. The gizzard gravy also tastes great over rice, mashed potatoes, grits, or biscuits. Spoon it over Boursin Cheese Grits (page 88), or use as an alternative to pork sausage for biscuits and gravy.

In a medium bowl, soak the chicken gizzards in the buttermilk and kosher salt for 15 minutes. Using a slotted spoon, transfer the gizzards to a sheet pan.

In a small bowl, mix the garlic powder, onion powder, seasoned salt, paprika, and cayenne pepper. Sprinkle this seasoning over the gizzards, cover the sheet pan with plastic wrap, and refrigerate the gizzards for 1 hour.

Wash the potatoes. With the skin on, cut the potatoes lengthwise into ½-inch-thick fries. Place the cut potatoes into a large bowl of cold water, cover, and refrigerate for 1 hour.

Place the flour in a shallow dish.

Remove the gizzards from the refrigerator and dredge them in the flour, then shake off any excess flour and set aside; reserve the dredging flour.

Fill a large cast-iron skillet with ½ inch of vegetable oil and heat to 350 degrees F. Fry the chicken gizzards in batches, turning them often until they are golden brown on all sides, 5 to 8 minutes. Use a slotted spoon to transfer the gizzards to a paper-towel-lined tray.

Reduce the oven temperature to 325 degrees F.

Pour off the oil and drippings from the skillet, leaving about 4 tablespoons oil remaining. Over medium heat, add the onions, garlic, shredded carrots, and celery to the drippings and cook for 5 minutes. Whisk in the leftover dredging flour and cook for 2 minutes, stirring continuously. Pour in 2 cups hot water and continue to stir for 5 minutes, or until the mixture thickens to a paste. Whisk in the chicken broth, cover, and cook for 15 more minutes. Add the Worcestershire sauce, bay leaves, and salt and pepper to taste. Cover the skillet, transfer to the oven, and cook for 3 hours, or until the gizzards are fork tender. Let the meat rest before serving.

Once the gizzards and gravy are removed from the oven, heat 4 inches of oil to 350 degrees F in a heavy-duty pot for frying (use an electric fryer if available).

Remove the cut potatoes from the refrigerator and pat dry. Working in batches, drop the potatoes in the hot oil and cook for 10 minutes, or until crisp and golden brown. Using a slotted spoon or tongs, transfer the fries to a paper-towel-lined tray. Repeat until all the fries are done. Sprinkle with salt and pepper.

To serve, place the fries in shallow dishes, spoon gravy over the fries, and top with cheese curds. Using tongs, carefully toss the cheese curds into the fries. Top with more gizzards and gravy. Garnish with sliced scallions, if desired.

DEEP-FRIED FISH BONE BRITTLE

SERVES 2 TO 4 AS A SNACK

10 fresh whiting bones (from your local fish market)

1 teaspoon kosher salt, plus more as needed

1½ cups finely ground cornmeal

1 teaspoon Lawry's Seasoned Salt

1 teaspoon garlic powder

1 teaspoon onion powder

¼ teaspoon cayenne pepper

Vegetable oil, for frying

Lemon wedges, for serving

Hot sauce of choice, for serving (optional)

For this recipe, you don't want your bones too clean. You want a little meat still left on after the fillets have been cut—ask your fishmonger. I prefer whiting because they're bigger and can be broken into smaller pieces after cooking. Fresh sardines and smelt are also delicate enough for this preparation, but do not substitue other fish.

The trick is to deep-fry the bones until they are extra-crispy and brittle enough to eat safely. They become a fish-flavored snack that's better than any potato chip—you won't be able to eat just one. This recipe is easy to scale up or down, and makes a surprising addition to any party table.

Rinse the fish bones and shake off any excess water. Sprinkle the bones with kosher salt and set aside for at least 10 minutes. Line a platter with paper towels.

In a large Dutch oven or heavy-bottomed pot, heat 4 inches of oil to 375 degrees F (get out your deep-fry thermometer).

In a shallow dish, mix together the cornmeal, seasoned salt, garlic powder, onion powder, and cayenne pepper.

Working with two or three at a time, roll the salted fish bones in the seasoned cornmeal, then lift the bones and lightly shake off the excess.

Transfer each batch to the hot oil and carefully fry the fish bones until extra crispy, brittle, and brown, 7 to 10 minutes. Transfer to the paper towels to drain and season immediately with more kosher salt. Repeat with the remaining bones.

Serve them hot with lemon wedges. The bones are spicy, but if you like more heat, pass around your favorite hot sauce.

Beef, Lamb, and Pork

Cocoa-Crusted Rack of Lamb

Baby Back Ribs with Sweet Tea Barbecue Sauce

Beef and Potato Empanadas (Picadillo Empanadas)

Beef Liver with Vidalia Onion Soubise

Coca Cola–Glazed Ham Hocks
with Kumquat Marmalade

Grilled T-Bone Steak
with Green Tomato Chimichurri

Manischewitz–Braised Beef Short Ribs
with Orange Gremolata

Cornflake-Crusted Pork Tenderloin

Salisbury Steak Scallopini

Harissa Lamb Ribs with Tomato-Cucumber Relish

Meatloaf Wellington with Sorghum Mustard

Pork Chops Smothered in Tomato-Sage Gravy

COCOA-CRUSTED RACK OF LAMB
With Dark Cherry Gravy

SERVES 8

4 medium lamb racks (about
    8 pounds total)
2 tablespoons tamarind paste
½ cup unsweetened cocoa
    powder
1 teaspoon Ethiopian mitmita
    spice (or berbere spice blend;
    see headnote)
1 teaspoon garlic powder
1 teaspoon onion powder
1½ teaspoons Lawry's Seasoned
    Salt
1 tablespoon smoked paprika
¼ cup packed light brown sugar
Dark Cherry Gravy (page 179),
    for serving

Kansas City, where I was born, is rightly known worldwide for its barbecue. It used to be that on every barbecue menu you would find mutton, the meat of an adult sheep. Mutton is strong in taste, and maybe that's why it lost popularity and is now difficult to find. This technique for smoking lamb creates, in my opinion, the best-tasting barbecue you will ever have.

I experimented with other cuts of lamb to try to re-create the delicious barbecue I grew up with, and this is the closest I've come yet to the flavor of those childhood memories. The sweet-tart tamarind and the mitmita spice's blend of bird's eye chili peppers, cloves, and cardamom, among other ingredients, balance the mutton's gamy notes (look for mitmita online from specialty purveyors or try berbere seasoning as a substitute). It is perfect for an elegant dinner entrée or a cocktail party. Don't take my word for it: I have won many accolades and awards with this recipe.

In addition to the Dark Cherry Gravy, the lamb also pairs well with Sweet Tea Barbecue Sauce (page 168).

Carefully trim the excess fat from the racks. Keep in mind that retaining some fat does add to the flavor, so be careful not to over trim. Rub the tamarind paste over each rack.

Thoroughly mix together the remaining ingredients for the cocoa crust. Sprinkle the lamb racks with the mixture, making sure to cover all sides well. Transfer the seasoned racks to a large resealable plastic bag and refrigerate for 12 to 24 hours.

When ready to cook the lamb, prepare a charcoal grill, arranging coals more heavily in the center and lighter on the side. This will create a two-zone surface for grilling, with high heat in the center and a cooler zone around the edge. (You can do these racks on a gas grill as well, but I prefer the additional flavor and char you get from a charcoal grill.)

Lightly spray the grate with nonstick cooking spray or rub with vegetable oil and place over the coals to heat. Once the coals are hot, put the racks on the grill, meat side down, in the center of the grate over high heat to achieve a sear. Be mindful of flare-ups so the meat does not burn. Grill for 5 to 6 minutes on each side, until well browned, then transfer the racks to the low-heat zone around the edge of the grate and cover the grill.

Continue cooking, covered, for about 15 minutes, until the internal temperature of the lamb is 140 to 145 degrees F for medium rare (longer if you prefer it more done). Let the racks rest for 5 to 10 minutes before cutting into the ribs. Serve with dark cherry gravy.

BABY BACK RIBS
With Sweet Tea Barbecue Sauce

SERVES 4 TO 6

BRINE

1 gallon unsweetened brewed
  tea
2 cups packed brown sugar
½ cup kosher salt
¼ cup whole black peppercorns
3 bay leaves
5 cloves garlic, smashed
2 slabs baby back ribs (3 to 4
  pounds total)

SPICE RUB

1 tablespoon smoked paprika
2 teaspoons onion powder
2 teaspoons garlic powder
1 tablespoon packed brown sugar
½ teaspoon cayenne pepper
1 teaspoon chili powder
1 teaspoon ground cumin
1 cup Sweet Tea Barbecue Sauce
  (page 168), plus more for
  serving

The sweet tea brine imparts a subtle flavor of tea to the ribs that is enhanced by the barbecue sauce. Instead of making the spice rub, try your favorite low-sodium barbecue spice blend instead, if you choose. The Sweet Tea Barbecue Sauce can be made ahead of time and refrigerated until ready to use.

You will need to prepare part of this recipe a full day ahead of serving, so plan your cooking time with that in mind.

MAKE THE BRINE: In a large saucepan over medium heat, bring the tea almost to a simmer. Stir in the sugar, salt, peppercorns, bay leaves, and garlic and continue to cook until the sugar dissolves, but do not let the mixture boil. Set the pan aside to cool slightly for 10 minutes, then pour the brine into a large bowl, cover with plastic wrap, and refrigerate for at least 4 hours. Refrigerated brine can last for 7 to 10 days before using.

After 4 hours, cut each slab of ribs in half and add to the brine. Cover with plastic wrap and marinate in the refrigerator for 18 to 24 hours. Remove the ribs from the brine and pat dry.

MAKE THE SPICE RUB: Combine the spices in a bowl and mix well. Rub the ribs with the mixture to coat. The spice rub can be made ahead and kept in an airtight container in the refrigerator for up to 2 weeks.

Prepare your charcoal grill by placing coals on only one side of the grill to create a two-zone surface. Place the ribs on the side without the coals, and cook over indirect heat (250 to 300 degrees F) for about 2 hours, turning often, until well browned. Brush the ribs with the barbecue sauce once every 15 minutes or so before taking them off the grill, reserving any remaining sauce.

The ribs are done when the meat is tender and slightly pulls away from the bone. I use tongs to test by picking up a slab and gently bouncing it to see if the meat pulls away easily. Serve with sweet tea barbecue sauce passed separately.

BEEF AND POTATO EMPANADAS
(Picadillo Empanadas)

MAKES 12 TO 18 EMPANADAS

DOUGH
4½ cups all-purpose flour, plus
    more for dusting
2 teaspoons kosher salt
1 cup (2 sticks) unsalted butter,
    chilled
1 tablespoon white vinegar
2 large eggs

FILLING
4 tablespoons vegetable oil,
    plus enough for frying
1 cup finely chopped onion
6 cloves garlic, minced
½ cup finely chopped red pepper
½ cup finely chopped green
    pepper
½ cup shredded carrots
1½ cups potatoes peeled and
    cut into small dice
1½ pounds ground beef
1 teaspoon ground cumin
1 teaspoon ground cinnamon
1 teaspoon ground cloves
½ cup sliced green olives with
    pimentos
½ cup raisins
1 (8-ounce) can tomato sauce
¼ cup dry white wine
1 teaspoon Tabasco sauce
2 teaspoons chopped fresh
    oregano
2 bay leaves
Salt and pepper
Vegetable oil, for frying

Green Tomato Chimichurri
    (page 178), for serving

At a little street-food stand on the side of the road in Puerto Rico, I tasted my first picadillo, which is similar to a beef hash and usually served with rice and beans. The flavors were delicious and some of the spices I recognized, like cinnamon and cloves, were unfamiliar used in such a savory dish. The picadillo became an obsession as I traveled through other Latin countries. I discovered subtle differences: Some cultures added capers, boiled eggs, or spicy peppers, but the practice of using ground beef is pretty common. I found the most interesting use of the picadillo to be a filling for empanadas—a great comfort food that is both inexpensive and playful. Perfect for a party snack.

The empanada dough can be made 1 to 2 days in advance, and the empanadas can be assembled hours ahead and refrigerated until you are ready to fry.

MAKE THE DOUGH: Sift the flour and salt into a large bowl. Using a pastry cutter, cut the butter into the flour until it looks like pea-size crumbs.

In a small bowl, beat together the vinegar, eggs, and ¾ cup of ice water. Make a well in the center of the flour and pour the egg mixture into the well, using a fork to mix. Stir the mixture with the fork until a dough just begins to form. Add more ice water as needed to ensure the flour is moist, but not sticky.

Turn out the dough onto a lightly floured surface and knead gently, once or twice—just enough to bring the dough together. Form the dough into a flat rectangle, cover with plastic wrap, and refrigerate for at least 1 hour or up to 4 days. While the dough is chilling, prepare the filling.

MAKE THE FILLING: Heat 4 tablespoons oil in a large skillet over medium-high heat. Add the onion, garlic, and both peppers and sauté for 5 minutes, or until the vegetables soften and just start to brown. Stir in the carrots, potatoes, and ground beef and cook for 10 to 15 minutes, stirring occasionally, until the beef has browned.

Drain excess fat from the skillet, and add the cumin, cinnamon, cloves, olives, raisins, tomato sauce, white wine, Tabasco, oregano, and bay leaves. Reduce the heat to low, cover, and simmer for 20 to 25 minutes, until the mixture thickens. Add salt and pepper as needed. Remove from the heat and let cool.

To assemble, divide the chilled dough into thirds and place on a lightly floured work surface. Roll each portion out 1/8 inch thick. Using a round 6-inch cookie cutter, cut out 3 to 4 discs, gathering scraps to reroll as necessary to yield 12 to 18 discs.

Add 3 to 4 tablespoons filling to each disc and fold the dough over to enclose the filling. Use a fork to press and seal the edges closed. Repeat for the remaining empanadas.

Heat 1½ inches of oil in a heavy skillet over medium-high heat until it registers 350 degrees F on a deep-fry thermometer. Add the empanadas a few at a time, being careful not to crowd the pan, and fry for 6 to 7 minutes, until golden brown, turning once or twice. Transfer to a paper-towel-lined plate to drain before serving. Serve with green tomato chimichurri.

BEEF LIVER
With Vidalia Onion Soubise

SERVES 8

3 pounds beef liver, thinly sliced
2½ cups buttermilk
6 tablespoons unsalted butter,
    divided
4 large Vidalia onions, cut in half
    and thinly sliced
1¾ cups heavy cream
Salt and ground white pepper

BREADING
3 cups all-purpose flour
1 teaspoon Lawry's Seasoned
    Salt
1 teaspoon onion powder
1 teaspoon garlic powder
½ teaspoon freshly ground black
    pepper

This recipe represents the meeting of soul food and French cuisine—it's my souped-up version of the standard liver and onions. The soubise is a very classic, very versatile French sauce that dates back to Escoffier in the early 1900s. It can be served with meats and poultry. I chose it as a great sauce to balance out the flavor of the liver.

Notice that the onions are cooked twice in this recipe—once to season the butter that the liver is cooked in, and then removed and used to finish the onion soubise. Although the recipe calls for Vidalia onions, which are only available a few months out of the year in the spring, any sweet onion may be substituted.

Combine the liver with the buttermilk in a medium bowl. Cover with plastic wrap and refrigerate for at least 2 hours or overnight.

In a large skillet over medium heat, melt 4 tablespoons butter. Add the onions and sauté for 5 to 7 minutes, until soft. Remove the skillet from the heat and set aside.

In a medium skillet over low heat, melt the remaining 2 tablespoons butter. Use tongs to transfer the softened onions to this skillet and cook, stirring frequently, for 15 minutes, or until the onions are completely softened but not browned; reserve the original skillet with the butter. Stir in the cream and simmer for 5 to 7 minutes, until the mixture begins to thicken. Add salt and white pepper to taste. Transfer the onion mixture to a food processor and puree until the sauce is smooth. Set aside while you cook the liver.

MAKE THE BREADING: In a shallow dish, stir together the flour, seasoned salt, onion powder, garlic powder, and black pepper.

Return the original skillet with the butter to medium heat. Remove the liver from the buttermilk, and dredge each piece in the seasoned flour. Place the liver, a few pieces at a time, into the heated butter, being sure not to over-crowd. Cook for 3 to 5 minutes on each side, turning with tongs, until the liver is well browned on both sides. Transfer the cooked liver to a platter and repeat the process until all the liver is cooked.

Return all the browned liver to the large skillet, top with the onion soubise sauce, cover, and cook over medium heat for 5 minutes. Serve with rice or creamy potatoes.

COCA COLA–GLAZED HAM HOCKS
With Kumquat Marmalade

SERVES 6

6 smoked ham hocks (5 to 6 pounds total)

3 tablespoons vegetable oil

4 cloves garlic, smashed

1 cup coarsely chopped onion

4 teaspoons minced fresh ginger

2 teaspoons Chinese five-spice powder

2 whole star anise

1 tablespoon dry mustard

4 cups diet cola (see headnote)

1 cup Kumquat Marmalade (page 180), divided

1 teaspoon red pepper flakes

1 tablespoon finely chopped cilantro

In this country the pork, or ham hock was historically considered a castoff in fine kitchens, and was one of the cuts offered to the servants and slaves, or simply discarded as trash. Later, these cheap, common cuts were among the few options for thrifty cooks whose creativity and ingenuity led them to fashion recipes and techniques that turned ham hocks into a staple of today's soul cooking. Similarly, the less affluent in many other cultures throughout the world have enjoyed this cut for centuries. My travels through Asia exposed me to many new ways to cook ingredients I thought I knew well, and this recipe is one such example. Dining in a friend's home, I was amazed by the sticky-sweet sauce that clung to those braised ham hocks. When I returned to Atlanta, I searched for a way to recreate those flavors. The richness of the smoked hock marries well with the spices, and the cola (I use diet because the classic is too sweet) reduces to a syrupy sauce that accents the pork perfectly.

To remove some of the salt from the smoked ham hocks, place them in a large stockpot with enough water to cover. Bring to a simmer over medium heat and cook for 1 hour, adding water as necessary to keep the ham hocks covered. With a slotted spoon or tongs, carefully remove the hocks from the water to a baking sheet and pat dry with paper towels. Set aside.

Preheat the oven to 350 degrees F.

Heat the vegetable oil in a Dutch oven or heavy-bottomed pot over medium-high heat. When the oil is hot, add the garlic, onions, and ginger, and sauté for 2 to 3 minutes, until the onions are translucent. Stir in the five-spice powder, star anise, dry mustard, diet cola, ½ cup of the marmalade, the red pepper flakes, and cilantro. Reduce the heat to low, and simmer for 15 minutes. Add ham hocks and enough water to cover. Cover with the lid, transfer to the oven, and cook for 2½ to 3 hours, until the meat is fork tender.

Transfer the ham hocks to a broiler rack lined with foil. Strain the liquid from the Dutch oven into a medium saucepan, discarding the solids. Set the saucepan over medium heat and simmer for 30 minutes, or until the liquid becomes syrupy. Remove from the heat and whisk in the remaining ½ cup marmalade.

Preheat the broiler. Return the ham hocks to the oven, about 6 inches from the heating element, and broil for 5 to 7 minutes, until the skin begins to char slightly. Transfer to a serving platter and top with the marmalade syrup. Serve with bitter greens, such as arugula, dandelion greens, or turnip greens.

GRILLED T-BONE STEAK
With Green Tomato Chimichurri

SERVES 6

6 (24-ounce) T-bone steaks, about 1½ inches thick (I prefer certified Angus beef)
2 tablespoons kosher salt
1 tablespoon freshly cracked black pepper
2 teaspoons onion powder
2 teaspoons garlic powder
1 teaspoon paprika
1 teaspoon ground coriander
1 teaspoon ground allspice
½ teaspoon ground turmeric
Green Tomato Chimichurri (page 178), for serving

Grilling is the art of cooking food quickly over direct heat at a high temperature. This recipe is a simple introduction to preparing a perfect piece of meat. It starts with a good cut of meat, balanced seasoning, and I love to add a complementary sauce. I prefer to use T-bone steak, because it's like getting two steaks in one—a strip steak and a tenderloin steak. The meat is enhanced by simple seasoning, and a Latin-influenced sauce made using a traditional Southern staple: green tomatoes. I prefer charcoal grilling over gas because of the additional flavor that charcoal provides. Using a digital meat thermometer can help you avoid overcooking your steaks. Removed from the heat, the steaks effectively continue to cook while resting, the internal temperature rising at least 3 to 6 more degrees via carryover heat.

Place the steaks on a sheet pan. In small bowl, stir together the salt, pepper, onion powder, garlic powder, paprika, coriander, allspice, and turmeric. Rub the steaks with the seasoning mixture to coat, cover with plastic wrap, and refrigerate for at least 2 hours and up to 4 hours to marinate.

About 30 to 45 minutes before grilling, remove the steaks from the refrigerator to let them come up to room temperature.

Prepare the grill for direct cooking over medium-high heat, distributing the coals evenly. If using a charcoal grill, the grill is ready when the charcoal turns white. You should be able to hold your hand about 6 inches above the grill for 4 to 5 seconds when the coals are ready. You will grill the steaks with the grill uncovered, from start to finish.

Spray the grate with nonstick cooking spray, set it in place over the coals, and let the grate heat for 10 minutes. Place the steaks on the grill and leave them in place for 5 minutes to sear. Using long tongs, lift the steaks and rotate them 90 degrees to make grill marks. Cook for another 4 minutes, then flip the meat and grill on the other side for 4 to 8 minutes, until the meat reaches your desired temperature.

Use a meat thermometer to check doneness: 135 degrees F for medium-rare, 140 for medium, and 145 for medium-well. Transfer the steak to a clean sheet pan to rest for 8 to 10 minutes before slicing and serving. Serve with green tomato chimichurri.

MANISCHEWITZ–BRAISED BEEF SHORT RIBS *With Orange Gremolata*

SERVES 8

6 pounds bone-in beef short
   ribs, cut into 3- to 4-inch pieces
1 tablespoon Lawry's Seasoned
   Salt
1 tablespoon freshly cracked
   black pepper
2 teaspoons garlic powder
2 teaspoons onion powder
2 cups all-purpose flour, divided
¾ cup vegetable oil
5 cups beef broth
3 cups Manischewitz Concord
   Grape wine
2 cups chopped carrots
1 cup coarsely chopped celery
2 cups coarsely chopped onion
6 cloves garlic, smashed
1 (6-ounce) can tomato paste
Salt and pepper

GREMOLATA
¼ cup orange zest (from 2
   medium oranges)
2 tablespoons minced sundried
   tomato
2 cups finely chopped flat-leaf
   parsley
2 cloves garlic, minced

My grandmother was a quiet woman who raised her family, cooked daily, and attended Baptist church on Sunday. I have no recollection of her having much of a social life, other than chatting with the neighbors across the way from her front porch. She was quiet, humble, and never a drinking woman, but every week she would partake in a glass of the sweet red wine called Manischewitz. It tasted like grape juice to me. According to her, it was essential for the proper maintenance of an aging woman's blood. I'm not sure where this idea came from, but in her honor, I decided to explore the use of this wine in cooking. This recipe has turned out to be one of my favorites. It's sweet and savory and the acidity and tartness of the gremolata cuts through the sweetness of the wine to perfectly balance the richness of the short ribs.

Note in your planning that the short ribs need to marinate for 24 hours before cooking. The short ribs, like any braised meat, can be finished in a slow cooker if available.

The day before you plan to cook, place the short ribs in a large bowl. In a small bowl, stir together the seasoned salt, pepper, garlic powder, and onion powder. Rub the short ribs thoroughly with the seasoning mixture, cover with plastic wrap, and refrigerate for 24 to 36 hours.

The next day, put the short ribs in a large bowl and toss with ¾ cup of the flour to coat.

In a large skillet, heat the vegetable oil over medium heat until shimmering. Add the short ribs, a few at a time, and brown for 5 to 6 minutes per side, until the short ribs are evenly browned. Transfer the short ribs to a large deep baking dish or roasting pan, reserving the hot oil in the skillet.

Preheat the oven to 350 degrees F.

Whisk the remaining 1¼ cups flour, a small amount at a time, into the hot oil left in the skillet to form a roux. Continue to whisk until the roux turns a caramel brown color. Slowly whisk in the beef broth, followed by the wine. Continue to whisk until the broth is smooth and free of lumps. Simmer for about 10 minutes, stirring occasionally, until slightly thickened.

Stir in 2 cups water, the carrots, celery, onions, garlic, and tomato paste. Simmer for 10 more minutes, then taste and season with salt and pepper as needed. Pour the broth mixture over the short ribs in the baking pan. Cover with aluminum foil and bake for 3 to 3½ hours, until the meat is fork tender.

MAKE THE GREMOLATA: Mix the zest, sundried tomatoes, parsley, and garlic in a small bowl. Cover and refrigerate until you're ready to serve. The gremolata can be made ahead and kept, covered, in the refrigerator, for up to 2 days.

To serve, spoon the gremolata over the short ribs and pass the gravy on the side.

CORNFLAKE-CRUSTED PORK TENDERLOIN

SERVES 12

6 pounds pork tenderloins,
about 6 (remove any silverskin
or ask your butcher to trim it
away)
3 large eggs
¼ cup buttermilk
4 cups crushed cornflakes
1 teaspoon herbes de Provence
2 teaspoons garlic powder
2 teaspoons onion powder
2 teaspoons Lawry's Seasoned
Salt
1 teaspoon kosher salt
1 teaspoon freshly cracked black
pepper
Apple-Cranberry Mostarda
(page 184), for serving

This is a creative yet simple preparation for a nice dinner party. The tenderloin is considered the filet mignon of pork. Though lean, it is naturally tender and moist, lending itself to many preparations. In the Midwest it is often flattened, then breaded and fried and served on a sandwich with mustard, pickles, and onions. This recipe takes that classic preparation in a more elegant direction. Serve it with Apple-Cranberry Mostarda for a perfect sweet-tart pairing.

Preheat the oven to 375 degrees F.

In a wide shallow dish, whisk together the eggs and buttermilk until blended. In a separate shallow dish, mix the cornflakes and herbes de Provence.

In a small bowl, stir together the garlic powder, onion powder, seasoning salt, kosher salt, and black pepper. Sprinkle the pork tenderloins with the seasoning mixture, rubbing it into the meat as you go.

Roll the pork in the egg mixture, then in the cornflake mixture to coat. Place the breaded tenderloins on a baking sheet, cover with plastic wrap, and refrigerate for 30 minutes.

Remove from the refrigerator and transfer the tenderloins to a rack set in a baking sheet. Bake until a meat thermometer placed in the center of the meat reads 145 degrees F, about 25 minutes. Remove from the oven and let the meat rest for 10 minutes before slicing. Serve with mostarda on the side.

SALISBURY STEAK SCALLOPINI

SERVES 8

4 pounds hanger steak
1 teaspoon kosher salt
1 teaspoon freshly cracked black pepper
1 teaspoon onion powder
1 teaspoon garlic powder
1½ cups all-purpose flour
4 tablespoons unsalted butter
¼ cup extra-virgin olive oil
1 onion, thinly sliced
12 to 15 shiitake mushrooms, cleaned, stemmed, and sliced (about 1 cup)
3 cups beef broth
2 tablespoons ketchup
2 tablespoons Worcestershire sauce
1 tablespoon dry mustard

If you grew up in the United States after the end of World War II, you've most likely enjoyed Salisbury steak and even consider it a comfort food—I know I do. Hanger steak is often considered a less desirable cut, but despite this reputation, it's sometimes called the "butcher's secret" because it's ideal for quick cooking over high heat, such as grilling. This is an inexpensive, easy dish perfect for a weekday meal or informal gathering. Scallopini is a classic Italian technique for cooking thinly sliced cuts of meat, paired here with a traditional, American-style gravy and an uncommon cut of meat that's very rich in flavor. It's the best of all worlds.

Slice the hanger steak against the grain into 1½-inch-wide medallions. Lay a long piece of plastic wrap on a cutting board. Place a few steak medallions on the plastic, spacing them 2 to 3 inches apart. Cover the medallions with another piece of plastic wrap. Using a meat mallet, pound each medallion to an even thickness of about ¼ inch, being careful not to tear the meat.

In a small bowl, mix the salt, pepper, onion powder, and garlic powder. Season both sides of the medallions, pressing the seasoning to adhere to the meat. Place the flour in a shallow bowl and add any leftover seasoning to the flour. Dredge each medallion in the flour, shaking off any excess. Arrange the medallions in a single layer on a clean sheet pan. Reserve the excess flour for making the gravy.

In a large cast-iron skillet over medium heat, melt the butter with the olive oil. After 4 to 5 minutes, just before the fat begins to smoke, lay about half of the medallions in a single layer in the hot

oil. Cook for 2 minutes or until golden brown, then turn and brown on the other side, about 2 minutes. Transfer to a paper-towel-lined plate to drain. Repeat the process to brown all of the steak medallions.

Add the sliced onions and mushrooms to the skillet and sauté for 3 minutes, or until the onions are translucent. Using a whisk, stir the excess flour into the skillet until well blended. Reduce the heat to medium and whisk in the beef broth, ketchup, Worcestershire sauce, and dry mustard. Simmer the gravy for about 20 minutes, until thick.

Add the browned medallions back to the gravy and simmer for 2 minutes, then serve with Grandma Lue's Spinach Rice (page 94) or potatoes.

HARISSA LAMB RIBS
With Tomato-Cucumber Relish

SERVES 8

RIBS
1 tablespoon kosher salt
¼ cup harissa powder, plus
   more for serving
1 tablespoon garlic powder
1 tablespoon onion powder
1 tablespoon ground cumin
½ teaspoon red pepper flakes
¾ cup fresh lemon juice (from
   about 3 lemons), divided
2½ to 3 pounds bone-in lamb
   ribs, trimmed of fat cap and
   scored
4 cups beef broth
1 carrot, coarsely chopped
1 celery stalk, coarsely chopped
5 cloves garlic, smashed
1 small onion, coarsely chopped

TOMATO-CUCUMBER RELISH
2 cups chopped fresh Roma
   tomatoes
1 cup coarsely chopped seedless
   English cucumber
½ cup chopped flat-leaf parsley
¼ cup chopped fresh mint
2 cloves garlic, minced
¼ cup red wine vinegar
¼ cup extra-virgin olive oil
½ teaspoon kosher salt
½ teaspoon freshly cracked
   black pepper

Lamb ribs are often sold in stores as lamb breast. I discovered this affordable cut one day in the meat section at Walmart, and have been creating dishes with them every since. The meat is fatty, so slow cooking is required to render the fat, but it's worth the time to reveal the full flavor and velvety texture of this cut. It is very similar to pork belly. Note that the final preparation includes grilling.

The presence of spicy harissa adds a rich, gentle heat to the recipe. These ribs make a great appetizer or group starter, and can be braised days in advance and finished on the grill just before serving.

MAKE THE RIBS: At least one day before you plan to grill, prepare the marinade. In a small bowl, stir together the salt, harissa, garlic powder, onion powder, cumin, red pepper flakes, and ½ cup of the lemon juice. Rub generously all over the lamb ribs to coat. Place the ribs in a resealable plastic bag and refrigerate for at least 24 hours or up to 2 days.

When you are ready to cook, preheat the oven to 325 degrees F.

Transfer the ribs to a roasting pan. Add the beef broth, carrots, celery, garlic, and onion to cover the ribs. Cover the baking pan tightly with foil and roast for 1 to 1½ hours, until the meat is tender.

MAKE THE RELISH: While ribs are in the oven, prepare the tomato-cucumber relish. In a medium bowl, combine the tomatoes, cucumbers, parsley, mint, garlic, vinegar, remaining ¼ cup lemon juice, the olive oil, salt, and pepper and toss to mix. Cover the bowl with plastic wrap and refrigerate until ready to serve.

When ready to serve, transfer the cooked ribs to a platter or sheet pan to cool.

Pour the remaining broth into a medium saucepan and cook over medium heat for 30 to 45 minutes, stirring occasionally, until the liquid is reduced by half.

Prepare your grill for direct heat, or preheat a gas grill to 400 degrees F. Place the ribs on the grill and cook for 4 to 5 minutes, until slightly charred, then turn the ribs and grill the other side for 4 minutes to brown. Brush the ribs with the reduced broth and transfer to a cutting board. Let them rest for 5 minutes, then slice the ribs. Brush the ribs again with the reduced broth and sprinkle with a little more harissa before serving. Serve the ribs with the chilled tomato–cucumber relish.

MEATLOAF WELLINGTON
With Sorghum Mustard

SERVES 6

2 pounds ground chuck
1 teaspoon Lawry's Seasoned
   Salt
1 teaspoon freshly cracked black
   pepper
2 teaspoons onion powder
2 teaspoons garlic powder
1 teaspoon kosher salt
4 tablespoons unsalted butter
1 cup diced onion
½ cup diced celery
½ cup diced red pepper
1 cup minced oyster mushrooms
   (about 8 ounces)
2 cups packaged seasoned
   breadcrumbs
4 large eggs, beaten
Salt and freshly cracked black
   pepper

MUSHROOM DUXELLES
2 tablespoons unsalted butter
½ cup finely chopped portobello
   mushrooms (about 5 ounces)
½ cup finely chopped button
   mushrooms (about 5 ounces)
½ cup finely chopped shiitake
   mushrooms (about 5 ounces)
1 shallot, minced
1 tablespoon chopped flat-leaf
   parsley
1 teaspoon kosher salt
1 teaspoon ground white pepper
1 tablespoon cognac
1 (3-ounce) can bloc de foie
   gras de carnard, seasoned
   with Armagnac, crumbled
2 sheets from one 7.3-ounce
   box frozen puff pastry, thawed
1 egg, beaten for egg wash

SORGHUM MUSTARD
1 cup whole grain mustard
½ cup mayonnaise
2 tablespoons sorghum
   molasses

Wrapping a meatloaf instead of beef tenderloin in puff pastry, along with mushroom duxelles and foie gras, may sound insane, but it works. Sorghum molasses was a staple of any humble table, but we know now that it's also very high in nutritional value and antioxidants and is less processed than other sweeteners. Comfort food, after all, isn't comfortable just because it's cheap, but also because it tastes great.

Preheat the oven to 400 degrees F.

In a large bowl, use your hands to mix the ground chuck, seasoned salt, black pepper, onion powder, garlic powder, and kosher salt.

In a skillet over medium heat, melt the butter, add the onion, celery, and red peppers, and sauté for 3 to 5 minutes, until the onion is translucent. Allow the skillet to cool for 10 minutes, then add the vegetable mixture to the bowl with the meat. Add the minced oyster mushrooms, breadcrumbs, and beaten eggs, season with salt and pepper, and gently mix with your hands, making sure everything is fully incorporated into the meat.

Use a tablespoon of the meatloaf mixture to make a small patty, test fry it in a little hot oil, and taste for seasoning. Add additional salt and pepper to the mixture if needed. Set aside.

MAKE THE MUSHROOM DUXELLES: In a medium saucepan, melt the butter over medium heat. Add the portobello, button, and shiitake mushrooms and sauté for 5 to 8 minutes, until the mushrooms have released their liquid and begun to brown. Stir in the shallot, parsley, salt, and white pepper and cook for 3 to 5 more minutes, until the shallot is tender. Add the cognac and cook for another 10 to 15 minutes, stirring occasionally, until the mixture has thickened. Remove the pan from the heat and stir in the foie gras crumbles.

Line a baking sheet with parchment paper. Divide the meatloaf mixture into 6 thick, even patties, about 5½ ounces each, and place them on the baking sheet, leaving space in between. Bake for 10 to 15 minutes, until a meat thermometer inserted into the thickest part of the meat reads 125 degrees F. Let rest on the baking sheet for 15 minutes.

Line another baking sheet with parchment paper. On a lightly floured surface, roll out each thawed puff pastry sheet to a 12 x 14-inch rectangle. Cut each rectangle in half to make 6 sheets (freeze any remaining sheets). In the middle of each half-sheet, place one parcooked meatloaf patty. Top each patty with 2 to 3 tablespoons of the mushroom duxelles mixture and spread the chopped mushrooms out evenly, pressing lightly to mold them onto the patty. Gather the four corners of the puff pastry half-sheet over the patty, and twist the edges to seal tightly, pinching with your fingers to form a tight bundle. Place on the parchment-lined baking sheet. Brush with the egg wash.

Bake for 20 to 25 minutes, until golden brown, and a meat thermometer inserted into the center of the meatloaf reads 160 degrees F. Let the Wellingtons rest on the baking sheet for at least 10 minutes before serving.

MAKE THE SORGHUM MUSTARD: While the Wellingtons rest, mix together the mustard, mayonnaise, and sorghum molasses. Leftover mustard can be kept in an airtight container in the refrigerator for up to 2 weeks.

To serve, spread 2 tablespoons sorghum mustard on each plate and top with 1 meatloaf Wellington.

PORK CHOPS
Smothered in Tomato-Sage Gravy

SERVES 6

1 cup all-purpose flour
1 teaspoon Lawry's Seasoned Salt
1 teaspoon kosher salt
1 teaspoon garlic powder
1 teaspoon onion powder
½ teaspoon freshly cracked black pepper
¼ teaspoon cayenne pepper
6 (6- to 8-ounce) pork chops
½ cup vegetable oil
1½ cups chicken broth
4 cloves garlic, minced
1 (14.5-ounce) can diced tomatoes
¼ cup chopped fresh sage
8 to 10 whole sage leaves, reserved for garnish

This dish comes from a friend of mine from Puerto Rico, except his version uses cilantro in place of the sage. I changed the herb—sage being a quintessential autumn flavor—to shift the dish more toward fall. Sage is a strong enough herb to subtly perfume and elevate the naturally sweet combination of good pork and ripe tomatoes. If you want to substitute cilantro for the sage and add a squeeze of lime, the chops will have a lighter flavor, which is great for a spring or summer meal.

Preheat the oven to 350 degrees F.

Place the flour in a shallow pan. In a small bowl, mix the seasoned salt, salt, onion powder, garlic powder, black pepper, and cayenne and rub onto the pork chops to season the meat. Stir any excess seasoning into the pan of flour.

Dredge the seasoned pork chops in the flour, shaking off any excess. Set the remaining flour aside for use in the gravy.

Heat the oil in a large cast-iron skillet over medium heat. Once the oil is hot, place 3 pork chops in the pan and brown for about 4 minutes on one side, then turn and brown for another 4 minutes on the other side, until evenly colored on both sides. Remove the pork chops to a paper-towel-lined plate to drain. Repeat with the remaining chops.

To make the gravy, pour off all but ¼ cup oil. Whisk the remaining flour into the drippings in the skillet over medium heat, until it forms a paste. Whisk in the chicken broth, garlic, and tomatoes and cook for 3 to 5 minutes, until the gravy thickens. Return the pork chops to the pan, reduce the heat to medium-low, and simmer for 5 minutes to let the flavors meld. Add the chopped sage and cover the skillet with a lid or foil.

Bake for 30 minutes, or until the meat is tender. If the gravy is too thick, stir in ¼ to ⅓ cup water and bake for another 5 minutes, covered. Remove from the oven and let the chops rest for at least 10 minutes. Garnish with the sage leaves, and serve with rice, noodles, potatoes, or dumplings.

Poultry

Candied Duck Wings with Apple-Cranberry Mostarda

Country Captain Chicken Stew

Pomegranate-Glazed Quail

Smoked Chicken and Pork Belly Brunswick Stew

Chicken and Sweet Potato Hash
with Chipotle Cream Sauce

Duck Prosciutto

Braised Chicken Wings Adobo with Coconut Gravy

Smothered Turkey Wings
with Cranberry-Apple Moonshine Gravy

Duck Schnitzel and Sweet Potato Waffles

Nashville Hot Turkey

Smothered Chicken Meatballs
over Herb-Truffle Spaetzle

CANDIED DUCK WINGS

With Apple-Cranberry Mostarda

SERVES 4 TO 6

DUCK WINGS

3 pounds duck drumettes
   (21 to 24)
1 tablespoon finely chopped
   fresh thyme
1 tablespoon finely chopped
   fresh rosemary
1 tablespoon finely chopped
   fresh basil
1 tablespoon finely chopped
   fresh tarragon
6 cloves garlic, smashed
1 teaspoon kosher salt
1 teaspoon Lawry's Seasoned
   Salt
1 tablespoon onion powder
1 tablespoon freshly cracked
   black pepper
32 ounces rendered duck fat
   (see headnote)
½ to 1 cup light olive oil, as
   needed

MAPLE CANDY GLAZE

½ cup maple syrup
½ teaspoon red pepper flakes
1 teaspoon freshly grated orange
   zest
1 teaspoon salt

Apple-Cranberry Mostarda
   (page 184), for serving

This is essentially a traditional confit, using duck wings instead of duck legs and thighs. No need to worry, a confit is super easy to make—it sounds exotic but it's really a combination of seasoned duck and duck fat, cooked slowly on low heat. It's important to know that you can re-use the leftover duck fat you've infused with herbs and garlic to sauté any vegetable, from asparagus to collard greens to potatoes.

Wings are an Atlanta specialty, good anywhere, anytime. I wanted to upgrade the basic recipe, so I use duck wings—a castoff, underutilized part of the duck, therefore inexpensive. I get mine at Your Dekalb Farmers Market, and I think a lot of farmers markets would offer them to you. You can substitute chicken wings—they won't take as long to bake—but the confit won't have quite the same deep flavor as the duck.

Leftover duck fat can be stored in a tightly covered container and refrigerated for up to 2 months, or frozen for up to 6 months.

MAKE THE DUCK WINGS: Preheat the oven to 250 degrees F.

In a large bowl, toss the duck wings with the herbs and smashed garlic. Stir together the salt, seasoned salt, onion powder, and black pepper and rub the wings thoroughly with the spice mixture to coat. Cover with plastic wrap and refrigerate for 3 hours, or overnight.

Melt the duck fat in a medium saucepan over low heat, then set aside to cool slightly, for ease in handling.

Arrange the marinated duck wings in a single layer in a baking dish. Pour the melted duck fat over the wings, adding the olive oil as needed to make sure the wings are completely covered with the fat. Cover and bake for 2 to 2½ hours, until the meat is tender enough to start pulling away from the bone. Remove from the oven and let the baking dish cool to room temperature.

Using tongs, carefully remove the wings from the fat and transfer to a broiler pan. Strain the fat and refrigerate for reuse (see headnote).

MAKE THE GLAZE: In a small saucepan, stir together the maple syrup, red pepper flakes, orange zest, and salt over low heat and simmer for 5 minutes, or until you see small bubbles appear around the edges of the pan.

Preheat the broiler to low. Generously brush the wings with the glaze, place the pan 4 to 5 inches from the heat, and broil for 3 to 5 minutes, until the wings are crispy (being careful not to let the sugar in the glaze burn). Serve immediately with the mostarda.

COUNTRY CAPTAIN CHICKEN STEW

SERVES 4

1 (2½- to 3-pound) chicken, cut
  into 8 pieces
1 teaspoon Lawry's Seasoned
  Salt
1 teaspoon onion powder
1 teaspoon garlic powder
½ teaspoon ground white pepper
2 tablespoons duck fat or
  unsalted butter
¾ cup chopped celery
½ cup chopped onion
½ cup chopped red bell pepper
½ cup chopped yellow bell
  pepper
2 cloves garlic, minced
2 cups chopped tomatoes (3 to
  4 medium)
½ teaspoon ground cinnamon
½ teaspoon ground cardamom
½ teaspoon red pepper flakes
2 tablespoons curry powder
4 sprigs fresh thyme
1 cup chicken broth
1 (13.5-ounce) can coconut milk
½ cup raisins
Salt and freshly ground black
  pepper

PEANUT RICE NOODLES
1 tablespoon vegetable oil
½ cup sliced scallions
1 (8.8-ounce) package rice
  noodles, cooked according to
  package directions, tossed in
  a little vegetable oil to prevent
  clumping, and chilled for 30
  minutes
1 teaspoon kosher salt
¼ cup chopped cilantro, plus
  more for garnish
½ cup toasted peanuts, plus
  more for garnish

This classic dish shows the influence of the Indian spice trade throughout the ports of the old South. It is typically served with rice and garnished with almonds, but I like to use rice noodles and peanuts—the rice noodles soak up the flavor perfectly, and the peanuts provide great texture and taste. This is one of those dishes that tastes better on the second day, so when possible, make it the day before serving. There are many different choices of curry powder, from sweet to the stronger flavors of Indian and Jamaican powder. I used a standard curry powder in this recipe, but if you like more heat, choose your preference.

Duck fat adds additional flavor to this stew—it's like cooking beans with bacon fat. It makes everything taste better (though you can substitute butter if you prefer)! No need to seek out specialty butchers: Duck fat can be purchased at Walmart or other supermarkets, or found online.

Preheat the oven to 350 degrees F.

In a large bowl, sprinkle the chicken pieces with the seasoned salt, onion powder, garlic powder, and white pepper. Cover the bowl with plastic wrap and refrigerate for 1 to 3 hours to marinate.

In a Dutch oven or heavy-bottomed pot over medium-high heat, melt the duck fat. When hot, add the chicken pieces and cook for 10 to 15 minutes, turning to brown on all sides. Transfer to a platter and set aside.

Add the celery, onion, peppers, and garlic to the fat remaining in the Dutch oven and cook for 3 to 5 minutes, until the onions are translucent. Add the tomatoes, cinnamon, cardamom, red pepper flakes, and curry powder, stir well to combine, and bring the mixture to a simmer. Return the chicken pieces to the pot, stir in the thyme, broth, coconut milk, and raisins, and season with salt and pepper. Cover, reduce the heat to medium-low, and simmer for 30 to 45 minutes, until the thighs are tender (the thighs usually take the longest to cook)

and the sauce has thickened.

MAKE THE NOODLES: While the chicken is simmering, prepare the noodles. Heat the vegetable oil in a skillet over medium heat and add the scallions and the chilled rice noodles. Cook for 3 to 5 minutes, tossing, until the noodles are heated through. Off the heat, add the salt, cilantro, and peanuts and toss to combine.

To serve, transfer the rice noodles to a wide bowl and ladle the chicken stew over the top. Garnish with additional peanuts and cilantro.

POMEGRANATE-GLAZED QUAIL

SERVES 8 AS AN APPETIZER

1 tablespoon Lawry's Seasoned
   Salt
2 teaspoons onion powder
2 teaspoons garlic powder
½ teaspoon ground white
   pepper
½ teaspoon ground cinnamon
8 (5- to 7-ounce) semi-boneless
   quail
2 tablespoons extra-virgin olive
   oil, divided

POMEGRANATE SYRUP
½ cup sugar
3 cups unsweetened
   pomegranate juice
2 teaspoons fresh lemon juice

When I was very young, I worked in a store that sold high-end men's gifts, which included wildlife prints, duck decoys, and other pricey hunting paraphernalia. I had never even tasted duck or pheasant or quail at that point, so I started to read everything I could about the flavor and preparation of these game birds that seemed so precious to hunters. I gained a love for cooking these fowl, but I still can't believe how much money people spend on duck decoys!

A tip: When reducing the pomegranate syrup, go slow and don't wander off. Reduced too far, it becomes pomegranate molasses, then hard candy.

This glaze is equally delicious on Cornish hens, chicken thighs or wings, cocktail wieners, meatballs, or even baby back ribs.

In a small bowl, stir together the seasoned salt, onion powder, garlic powder, white pepper, and cinnamon. Rub the quail inside and out with the seasoning mixture, transfer them to a baking sheet, cover with plastic wrap, and chill for at least 4 hours to marinate.

MAKE THE SYRUP: Combine the sugar, pomegranate juice, and lemon juice in a medium saucepan over medium heat. Stir occasionally until the sugar has dissolved, then reduce the heat to low and simmer for 50 to 60 minutes, until the syrup has reduced to about 1 cup.

Remove from the heat, cover, and let the syrup cool in the saucepan for at least 30 minutes.

Remove the upper rack from the oven and preheat the oven to 500 degrees F.

Remove the quail from the refrigerator and let it come to room temperature, still in the marinade, before cooking.

Spray a clean, rimmed baking sheet with vegetable oil and place the quail on it.

Heat 1 tablespoon of the olive oil in a large skillet over medium-high heat until just smoking. Add 4 quail to the

skillet and cook for 2 to 4 minutes on each side, until nicely browned. Return the browned quail, breast side up, to the baking sheet.

Add the remaining 1 tablespoon oil and repeat with the remaining quail. Return them, breast side up, to the baking sheet with the others.

Brush the quail evenly with half of the pomegranate syrup, and roast in the preheated oven for 8 to 10 minutes (semi-boneless quail doesn't take as long to cook as bone-in, and you don't want to overcook the meat). The quail is done when the meat is slightly firm to the touch and the juices run clear when you insert a fork.

Preheat the broiler. Remove the quail from the oven and brush with the remaining syrup. Return to the oven and broil for 5 to 7 minutes, until the quail are very well browned, even lightly blackened in spots, but not burned. Transfer to a serving platter and let rest for 5 minutes before serving.

SMOKED CHICKEN AND PORK BELLY BRUNSWICK STEW

SERVES 16 TO 20

¼ cup vegetable oil

4 tablespoons unsalted butter

2 cups coarsely chopped onion

1 cup coarsely chopped red bell pepper

1 cup coarsely chopped green bell pepper

1 cup coarsely chopped celery

5 cloves garlic, minced

2 pounds Smoked Pork Belly (recipe below), diced

8 cups chicken broth

1 (28-ounce) can diced tomatoes

1½ to 2 cups corn kernels, cut from about 4 corn cobs

1 (8.25-ounce) can creamed corn

2 cups frozen lima beans

3 large russet potatoes, peeled and cut into ½-inch cubes (about 3 cups)

2 cups Sweet Tea Barbecue Sauce (page 168), or your choice of brand

1 tablespoon liquid smoke

½ cup apple cider vinegar

2 tablespoons Worcestershire sauce

1 tablespoon Lawry's Seasoned Salt

2 teaspoons kosher salt

1 tablespoon onion powder

1 tablespoon garlic powder

Meat from 2 Smoked Chickens (recipe below), chopped or pulled

Salt and freshly ground black pepper

Brunswick stew is synonymous with comfort food in Georgia, the entire South, and beyond. Its wafting aroma while simmering fills my kitchen and my soul with warmth and memories of family gatherings in the fall. This is a hearty dish made with simple ingredients, and a guaranteed crowd-pleaser.

I suggest buying smaller chickens because the chickens that haven't been injected with hormones are smaller and healthier.

This recipe requires a charcoal grill or smoker and hickory chunks. (I prefer hickory for the flavor it imparts, but you can substitute your favorite wood.) It's a multi-stage dish so it's a commitment, but the results are so worth it. Smoking the chicken and pork belly in advance can get you halfway there sooner.

Because this is a time-consuming recipe, I always like to make a big batch and freeze half the stew. It will keep for up to 6 months in the freezer. If you prefer a smaller yield, this recipe works as well cut in half.

In a large Dutch oven or heavy-bottomed pot, heat the oil and butter over medium-high heat. Once shimmering, add the onion, red pepper, green pepper, celery, and garlic and sauté for 3 to 5 minutes, until the onion is translucent. Add the smoked pork belly, the chicken broth, and diced tomatoes. Bring to a boil, cover, and reduce the heat to low. Simmer for 30 minutes to cook the pork belly and meld the flavors, stirring occasionally to prevent sticking.

Stir the fresh corn kernels and all the remaining ingredients except the salt and pepper into the Dutch oven, cover, and simmer for another 30 to 45 minutes, stirring often, until the vegetables are tender and the smoked chicken is cooked through. Remove from the heat. Season with salt and pepper to taste.

SMOKED CHICKEN

2 (2½- to 3-pound) whole
  chickens, cut in half
2 teaspoons Lawry's Seasoned
  Salt
1 teaspoon kosher salt
2 teaspoons smoked paprika
2 teaspoons onion powder
2 teaspoons garlic powder
2 teaspoons freshly ground
  black pepper
1 teaspoon ground cumin
1 teaspoon chili powder
1 teaspoon cayenne pepper
3 tablespoons vegetable oil

SMOKED PORK BELLY

2 pounds pork belly, skin
  removed
1 tablespoon kosher salt
1 teaspoon Lawry's Seasoned
  Salt
1 tablespoon smoked paprika
1 teaspoon chili powder
½ teaspoon cayenne pepper

MAKE THE CHICKEN: Lay the chicken flat on a sheet pan. In a small bowl, stir together the seasoned salt, salt, paprika, onion powder, garlic powder, black pepper, cumin, chili powder, and cayenne and rub this seasoning mix over the chicken, and under the skin, on both sides. Transfer to a large resealable bag. Add the oil, seal the bag, and turn to distribute the oil over the chicken. Chill in the refrigerator for 1 hour.

MAKE THE PORK: At same time, lay the pork belly flat on another sheet pan and use a sharp knife to score the fat ¼-inch-deep in a diagonal diamond pattern.

In a small bowl, stir together the salt, seasoned salt, smoked paprika, chili powder, and cayenne. Rub the pork belly well on both sides with the seasoning. Transfer to a large resealable plastic bag and chill for 1 hour alongside the chicken.

Meanwhile, soak 4 or 5 hickory chunks in a bowl of water for 30 minutes.

Prepare your grill or smoker for low indirect heat by arranging a small amount of charcoal on one side. Light the coals and once they have turned white, place 2 soaked wood chunks on top and replace the grate.

Place the marinated chicken and pork belly on the cool side of the grill (opposite the coals), cover the grill, ensure the vents are slightly open to keep the heat low and smoke in, and smoke for 2 hours, adding more wood as needed and turning the meat when necessary to prevent burning. After 2 hours, the meat will be smoked, but not completely cooked, but it will finish cooking in the stew. Remove the chicken and pork from the coals and set aside to cool for 20 minutes.

Once cool, pull or cut the smoked chicken off the bone and shred with two forks (don't be concerned if the chicken is still pink); discard the bones and skin. Set aside.

Dice the smoked pork belly into small pieces and set aside.

If you are cooking a day ahead, place the chicken and meat in separate resealable plastic bags, or in covered containers, and refrigerate until ready to use, or up to 3 days.

CHICKEN AND SWEET POTATO HASH
With Chipotle Cream Sauce

SERVES 4 TO 6

HASH
½ teaspoon Tony Chachere's Original Creole Seasoning

1 teaspoon garlic powder

1 teaspoon onion powder

1 teaspoon Lawry's Seasoned Salt

4 boneless, skinless chicken thighs, cut into ½-inch cubes

2 cups fingerling sweet potatoes, peeled and cut into ½-inch cubes

3 tablespoons duck fat or light olive oil

½ cup finely diced onion

½ cup diced red bell pepper

1½ cups loosely packed chopped fresh kale

½ teaspoon freshly cracked black pepper

Pinch of kosher salt

CHIPOTLE CREAM
1 cup sour cream, at room temperature

1 whole canned chipotle pepper in adobo, or more if you want more heat

2 scallions (green tops only), sliced

½ teaspoon kosher salt

Poached or sunny-side up eggs, for serving

Flavorful chicken thighs pair well with sweet potato. I use fingerling sweet potatoes because they are especially sweet. The chipotle cream adds just the right amount of heat to make this dish sassy but well balanced. You can make the hash the day before and reheat before serving. It tastes great with or without the poached egg topping.

MAKE THE HASH: In a small bowl, blend the Creole seasoning, garlic powder, onion powder, and seasoned salt.

In a medium bowl, toss the cubed chicken with the seasoning mixture to coat. Cover with plastic wrap and refrigerate to marinate for at least 1 hour.

In a medium saucepan, bring the cubed sweet potatoes and enough hot water to cover to a boil over medium-high heat. Cook for 15 to 18 minutes, until the potatoes are firm but tender; do not overcook. Drain and set aside for about 10 minutes to cool.

In large sauté pan, heat the duck fat over medium just until shimmering. Add the onion and red pepper and cook for about 5 minutes, until the vegetables soften. Add the chicken to the pan and continue to cook for 10 to 15 minutes, stirring, until the chicken is well browned. Add the cooked fingerling sweet potatoes, chopped kale, black pepper, and salt and stir to combine. Reduce the heat to low and continue to cook for 8 to 10 more

minutes, stirring occasionally, until the kale wilts. Reduce the heat as low as you can get it to keep the hash warm while you make the chipotle cream.

MAKE THE CHIPOTLE CREAM: Combine the sour cream, chipotle pepper, scallion greens, and salt in a food processor and process until smooth, 1 to 2 minutes.

To serve, dish out a portion of hash and add a dollop of chipotle sour cream. Top with a poached or sunny-side up egg.

DUCK PROSCIUTTO

MAKES FOUR 6- TO 7-OUNCE PIECES

2 (16- to 18-ounce) whole duck
  breasts with skin, split in half
3 cups kosher salt
¼ cup packed brown sugar
½ teaspoon freshly cracked
  black pepper

I love all things charcuterie, but for years thought that the prosciutto-making process was too complicated for anyone except charcutiers or master butchers. While living for a short time in Siena, Italy, I learned a lot about curing some of the best hams in the world. I also learned a simpler process that could work on duck breasts, which are much easier to find than heirloom pigs. All it takes is a few key ingredients, some cheesecloth, butcher's twine, and a little time, and you will marvel over the results.

I make duck prosciutto every few months and use it in canapés and salads, or I pan-fry it and toss it with pasta. Serve it with hardy cheeses or as part of a charcuterie platter. I like to add head cheese, bologna mousse, pickled tomatoes, roasted red peppers, and pickled mustard seeds, which pair well with fatty meats. Once cured, the duck prosciutto can be wrapped in plastic and refrigerated for several weeks.

Rinse the duck under cold running water and dry well. Take out a glass baking dish just large enough to lay both breasts flat with no overlap.

In a medium bowl, mix the salt and brown sugar. Pour a 1-inch-deep layer into the bottom of the dish and place the duck breasts, skin side-up, on top of the salt mixture. Top the duck breasts with another 1-inch layer of the salt mixture, being sure to cover the breasts completely, and press down to pack solidly. Wrap the entire dish in plastic wrap and refrigerate for 24 hours, or up to 48 hours for a saltier proscuitto.

Unwrap the dish, remove the duck breasts from the salt mixture, and rinse thoroughly, then pat dry with paper towels. The cured duck will feel slightly drier and harder and its color will be darker. Dust each breast with cracked black pepper.

Wrap each breast tightly and completely in cheesecloth, then use butcher's twine to tie the cloth ends together, leaving a 4-inch string hanging from each wrapped bundle, long enough to hang the duck for curing. You can hang the duck bundles from a rack in the back of your refrigerator, or in a cool garage, cellar, or basement. The ideal temperature, if hanging outside of the refrigerator, is 50 to 60 degrees F. Allow the duck to hang for 10 to 21 days. At day 10, start testing by pressing to make sure the duck still holds moisture. The prosciutto is done when the duck breast feels firm, not dry and hard. If the duck becomes too dry, it will become more like jerky.

At the end of the curing time, remove the cheesecloth, wrap the prosciutto in plastic wrap, and refrigerate. To serve, slice it super thin.

BRAISED CHICKEN WINGS ADOBO
With Coconut Gravy

SERVES 6

4 pounds chicken wings (about
  20)
1 tablespoon light soy sauce
6 tablespoons vegetable oil,
  divided
½ tablespoon kosher salt
½ tablespoon garlic powder
½ tablespoon onion powder
1 teaspoon ground ginger
¼ cup coconut vinegar (see
  headnote)
6 cloves garlic, smashed
1 teaspoon grated fresh ginger
3 bay leaves
1 tablespoon whole black
  peppercorns
1 (13.5-ounce can) coconut milk

I had the opportunity to meet and work with a young woman from the Philippines. Nancy was incredibly talented in the kitchen, especially with simple, delicious sauces. One day for a potluck supper she brought this chicken dish, which featured preparations that reminded me of smothered chicken and gravy. Nancy explained that it was a dish from her childhood that her grandmother prepared regularly—one, I've since learned, is considered the national dish of the Philippines, chicken adobo.

Like the smothered chicken I grew up with, chicken adobo is typically served over rice. A quick discussion of the ingredients was all I needed to start preparing this recipe on my own. I chose chicken wings, but any part of the chicken will yield the same results—a delicious dish of super-tender chicken and deep flavor that's more than the sum of its parts. Coconut vinegar can be found online and in most Asian markets.

This is my take on the iconic dish of Nancy's homeland.

In a large bowl, toss together the chicken wings, soy sauce, and 2 tablespoons vegetable oil to coat. Sprinkle the salt, garlic powder, onion powder, and ginger over the wings and toss, then cover and refrigerate for at least 4 hours or overnight.

When you are ready to cook, heat the remaining 4 tablespoons vegetable oil in a large skillet over medium-high heat. Drain the wings, shaking off any excess liquid. When the oil just starts to smoke, carefully add the wings to the skillet, being careful not to crowd the pan (do it in batches, if necessary), and cook for 6 to 8 minutes, turning once, until well browned on both sides. Transfer to a platter, and repeat with the remaining wings.

Pour off any oil left in the skillet and return the pan to medium-high heat. Add 2 cups water and use a spoon or spatula to scrape up the browned bits from the bottom and sides of the skillet. Add the coconut vinegar, garlic, ginger, bay leaves, and peppercorns, reduce the heat to low, and simmer for 5 minutes.

Add the chicken wings back to the skillet, cover, and cook over low heat for 20 minutes. Stir in the coconut milk and simmer for an additional 10 to 15 minutes, until the gravy thickens and the wings are tender. Remove from the heat and set aside to rest for 10 minutes before serving. To serve, spoon over plain rice or noodles.

SMOTHERED TURKEY WINGS
With Cranberry-Apple Moonshine Gravy

SERVES 6

1 tablespoon Lawry's Seasoned
    Salt
1 tablespoon garlic powder
1 tablespoon onion powder
1 teaspoon freshly cracked black
    pepper
1 tablespoon herbes de Provence
12 turkey wings (7 to 8 pounds
    total)
1 cup all-purpose flour
¾ cup vegetable oil
4 tablespoons unsalted butter
5 cloves garlic, smashed
1 onion, chopped
½ cup chopped celery
3 cups chicken or turkey broth
1 cup apple cider
1 (14-ounce) can whole-berry
    cranberry sauce
1 teaspoon kosher salt
¾ cup White Lightnin'
    Moonshine (see headnote)
Cajun Cornbread Dressing
    (page 111), for serving

If you are looking for something different to serve for the holidays, this is your answer. Instead of a whole turkey, why not just prepare the wings—wings are a popular comfort food and, in this recipe, they are far juicier and tastier than the typical, dry holiday bird—plus no fighting over the drumsticks. As a special holiday bonus, the moonshine gravy is delicious enough to keep the conversation away from politics!

Ole Smoky White Lightnin' Moonshine adds a distinctive jolt to the sauce and is available widely in liquor stores and online. Make sure you have a well-ventilated space and keep a kitchen fire extinguisher handy.

In a small bowl, stir together the seasoned salt, garlic powder, onion powder, pepper, and herbes de Provence. Rub the seasoning all over the turkey wings. Place the flour in a large resealable plastic bag, add the seasoned turkey wings, and shake to coat the wings in the flour. Remove the wings to a wire rack set in a rimmed baking sheet and reserve the remaining flour.

Heat the oil and butter in a Dutch oven or heavy-bottomed pot over medium-high heat. Add 2 to 3 turkey wings, taking care not to crowd the pan, and cook for 8 to 10 minutes, turning once, until well browned. Transfer the browned wings to a large baking dish or pan and repeat with the remaining wings.

Once all the wings have been browned, stir the garlic, onion, and celery into the Dutch oven. Cook for 5 minutes, then whisk in the reserved flour and continue to whisk for 5 to 7 minutes, until the flour turns a golden brown. Whisk in the broth and apple cider, reduce the heat to medium, and simmer for 20 minutes, or until the mixture slightly thickens. Whisk in the cranberry sauce and kosher salt until well blended, then very carefully add the moonshine—be aware that the moonshine may ignite for a few seconds in the pan; just let it burn off. It will dissipate within seconds.

Pour the gravy over the turkey wings, cover tightly with foil, and bake for 2 to 2½ hours, until the wings are fork tender. Remove from the oven and set aside to rest for 10 minutes before serving.

To plate individual servings, top 2 wings with gravy and pass the Cajun cornbread dressing around the table.

DUCK SCHNITZEL AND SWEET POTATO WAFFLES

SERVES 8

4 large duck breasts (3½ to
    4 pounds), split in half, skin
    removed
1 tablespoon Lawry's Seasoned
    Salt
1 tablespoon onion powder
1 tablespoon garlic powder
1 tablespoon freshly cracked
    black pepper
½ cup all-purpose flour
4 large eggs
1½ cups panko breadcrumbs
1 tablespoon herbes de Provence
1 teaspoon kosher salt
Vegetable oil, for frying

SWEET POTATO WAFFLES
2 large sweet potatoes
1 cup milk
2 large egg yolks
4 tablespoons unsalted butter,
    melted
¼ cup packed light brown sugar
½ teaspoon ground cardamom
½ teaspoon vanilla extract
2 cups all-purpose flour
1 tablespoon baking powder
½ teaspoon ground cinnamon
½ teaspoon kosher salt
6 large egg whites

Cinnamon, Ginger, and Star
    Anise Butter (page 172), for
    serving
Bourbon Peach Jam (page 195),
    for serving

This combination blows plain old fried chicken and waffles clean out of the water! I've always liked duck with sweet potatoes. Duck is simply more flavorful than chicken, and when paired with a waffle that is sweeter than your ordinary brunch fare, the results are incredible. Pounding the duck breast out thin and breading it schnitzel-style tenderizes the meat and allows the flavors to penetrate throughout. It cooks quickly—just brown it and it's done—so it's a good dinner choice to prepare when you don't have much time.

Place each duck breast between two pieces of plastic wrap. Using a meat mallet, gently pound each duck breast about ¼ inch thick.

In a small bowl, stir together the seasoned salt, onion powder, garlic powder, and black pepper. Season both sides of each duck breast with the mixture, then transfer to a resealable plastic bag, and chill for at least 4 hours, or overnight, to marinate.

When ready to cook the duck, put the flour in a wide, shallow bowl. Beat the eggs together in a medium bowl. In a third bowl, stir together the breadcrumbs, herbes de Provence, and kosher salt.

Dredge each duck breast in the flour, dip in the beaten eggs, then roll in the breadcrumb mixture, pressing the breadcrumbs lightly with your fingers to coat. Transfer the breaded duck to a platter.

In a large skillet, heat ¼ inch vegetable oil over medium-high heat until shimmering. Add the breaded duck breasts, up to three at a time, to the hot oil. Cook for 2 to 3 minutes on each side, until golden brown. Transfer the cooked schnitzel to a paper-towel-lined tray to drain and repeat with remaining duck breasts.

While the duck breasts marinate, prepare the waffle batter.

MAKE THE WAFFLES: Preheat the oven to 400 degrees F.

Pierce the sweet potatoes with a fork and bake them, skin on, for 45 to 50 minutes, until fork tender. Set aside to cool, then use a knife to split open the tops and spoon the sweet potato flesh into a bowl and mash with a fork or potato masher.

In a large bowl, combine the mashed sweet potatoes, milk, egg yolks, melted butter, brown sugar, cardamom, and vanilla. Whisk together until well blended.

In another large bowl, stir together the flour, baking powder, cinnamon, and salt. Stir in the sweet potato mixture and blend well.

In another bowl, use a hand mixer to beat the egg whites to stiff peaks, about 1 minute on medium-high speed.

In three parts, gently fold the egg whites into the batter until well blended.

Preheat an 8-inch-diameter waffle iron. Once hot, spray the waffle iron with nonstick cooking spray. Working quickly, pour 1¼ cups batter into the waffle iron and spread the batter with an offset spatula. The mixture will be thick, so take care to spread it evenly to the edges. Close the waffle iron and cook for 3 to 5 minutes, until the waffle is golden and crisp and separates easily from the iron. Place on a plate and keep warm. Repeat with the remaining batter until you have 8 waffles in all.

To serve, split each sweet potato waffle in quarters, and top with 1 duck schnitzel. Serve with the compound butter and peach jam or your favorite syrup.

NASHVILLE HOT TURKEY

SERVES 8

1 tablespoon Lawry's Seasoned
  Salt
2 teaspoons garlic powder
2 teaspoons onion powder
4 pounds boneless turkey
  breast, sliced into 8 pieces
2 cups buttermilk
4 large eggs, beaten
½ cup hot sauce, your choice of
  brand
3 cups all-purpose flour
1 tablespoon kosher salt

SPICY OIL
½ cup (1 stick) unsalted butter,
  cut into cubes
½ cup vegetable oil
¼ cup packed dark brown sugar
1 teaspoon cayenne pepper
2 teaspoons garlic powder
2 teaspoons onion powder
1 teaspoon chili powder

Vegetable oil, for frying
8 slices white bread or Texas
  toast, for serving
Pickle slices, for serving

An African American dish from Nashville, the original recipe is said to come from a woman who put extra cayenne pepper on her womanizing boyfriend's chicken sandwich to get revenge. Instead, he liked it and by the mid-1930s he and his brother had created their own recipe and opened a chicken shack. Now it's considered a staple of late-night diners.

I substituted turkey breast for the chicken because I ordered too many turkeys one Thanksgiving and needed to do something different with one of the birds. It's really a glorified open-faced sandwich. If you're broke, it's a meal; if you're not, make some fries to go with it. Either way, you'll enjoy it.

This recipe needs to be started the day before you plan to serve.

In a small bowl, stir together the seasoned salt, garlic powder, and onion powder. Lay the turkey slices on a baking sheet and sprinkle with half of the seasoning mixture. Flip and sprinkle the other side with the remaining mixture. Cover with plastic wrap and refrigerate for at least 6 hours, or overnight. The next day, stir together the buttermilk, eggs, and hot sauce in a medium bowl. Set aside.

In a shallow bowl, mix the flour with the kosher salt. Dredge the seasoned turkey in the flour, then dip it in the buttermilk (letting the excess drip off), and then back through the flour again to coat. Lay each piece on a clean wire rack set in a baking sheet.

MAKE THE SPICY OIL: In a small saucepan over low heat, whisk together the butter, oil, brown sugar, cayenne, garlic powder, onion powder, and chili powder. Simmer over low heat for 5 minutes to let the flavors develop, then remove from the heat and set aside to cool.

In a large skillet, heat 1½ inches vegetable oil over medium-high until the oil reaches 350 degrees F. Add the turkey slices a few pieces at a time, making sure not to overcrowd the skillet. Fry for 10 to 15 minutes, turning occasionally, until the turkey is golden brown on both sides. Transfer to a wire rack to drain.

Brush each turkey breast with spicy oil. Serve over white bread or Texas toast, with pickles on the side.

SMOTHERED CHICKEN MEATBALLS
Over Herb-Truffle Spaetzle

SERVES 6

MEATBALLS
¼ cup milk
3 slices of bread, torn into small
    pieces
6 tablespoons unsalted butter,
    divided
1 small onion, finely chopped
½ red bell pepper, finely chopped
1 pound boneless, skinless chicken
    thighs, finely ground in a food
    processor
8 ounces skinless chicken
    breast fillets, finely ground in
    a food processor
1 large egg
1 teaspoon Lawry's Seasoned Salt
½ teaspoon freshly cracked
    black pepper
1 teaspoon garlic powder
1 teaspoon onion powder
¼ teaspoon ground nutmeg
Pinch of cayenne pepper
½ cup all-purpose flour
¼ cup vegetable oil

SMOTHERING GRAVY
1 yellow onion, thinly sliced
1 teaspoon kosher salt
½ teaspoon freshly cracked
    black pepper
2 cloves garlic, minced
½ cup all-purpose flour
1½ cups chicken broth, warmed
1 bay leaf

Spaetzle is a sort of German noodle or dumpling that's boiled then pan-fried until brown and crisp. I use a metal colander set over boiling water, although you can find spaetzle makers online or in specialty kitchenware stores (they look like cheese graters). My love for German dishes inspired me to create this version of chicken and dumplings. It's simple to make, the spaetzle is lighter and tastier than Southern dumplings, and it pairs well with the meatballs without overpowering the flavor of the chicken.

If you're trimming a chicken, you can use the scraps and castoffs instead of breasts and thighs. Just make sure you combine dark and white meat and run them through a food processor—or buy already ground chicken.

If you have granulated garlic or onion rather than the powdered version, you may substitute these. It will only affect the color of the meatball. Black truffles are easily purchased online, and they keep for 1 to 3 months in an airtight container in the freezer.

MAKE THE MEATBALLS: In a small bowl, pour the milk over the bread and press down with a spoon or your fingers so that the bread soaks up all the milk; set aside for 5 minutes.

In a large skillet, melt 2 tablespoons of the butter over medium heat, add the onions and red peppers, and cook for 3 to 5 minutes, until the onions are translucent. Transfer to a large bowl and set aside to cool.

When the onions and peppers have cooled, add the ground chicken, soaked bread, the egg, seasoned salt, black pepper, garlic powder, onion powder, nutmeg, and cayenne to the bowl and mix until just combined. Don't overmix or you'll get tough meatballs. Shape into 24 small or 12 large meatballs, as preferred, and place them on a tray or baking sheet. At this point, they can be covered and refrigerated for up to 24 hours.

When ready to cook, spread the flour in a shallow dish. Roll each meatball through the flour to coat, and set aside on a plate.

In a large skillet, heat the remaining 4 tablespoons butter and the vegetable oil over medium heat. Add the meatballs a few at a time and cook for 8 to 12 minutes (depending on the size of the meatballs), turning every couple of minutes, until browned on all sides. Transfer the browned meatballs to a paper-towel-lined plate to drain.

MAKE THE GRAVY: Add the sliced onions to the drippings in the skillet, add the salt and pepper, and return to medium heat. Cook, stirring occasionally, for 5 to 7 minutes, until the onions are a rich golden brown. Add the garlic and cook for 1 minute, or until fragrant. Whisk the flour into the onions and garlic and slowly add the chicken broth, whisking until all the broth is incorporated and the gravy

HERB–TRUFFLE SPAETZLE

2 cups all-purpose flour

4 large eggs, lightly beaten

⅓ cup milk

1 teaspoon kosher salt

½ teaspoon freshly cracked
  black pepper

1 tablespoon minced fresh
  thyme leaves

1 teaspoon minced flat-leaf parsley

1½ ounces black truffles, grated

1 teaspoon black truffle oil

1 tablespoon unsalted butter,
  softened

6 sprigs fresh thyme, for garnish

is smooth and free of lumps. Add the bay leaf. Reduce the heat to low and simmer for 8 to 10 minutes.

Add the meatballs to the gravy and continue to simmer over low heat for about 20 minutes while you make the spaetzle. If the gravy starts to get too thick, add more broth as desired to loosen it.

MAKE THE SPAETZLE: If you don't have a spaetzle maker, choose a pot that your colander (one with big holes will make things easier) fits in securely. In your spaetzle maker or pot, bring 8 cups salted water to a boil over medium-high heat.

In a large bowl, stir together the flour, eggs, milk, salt, pepper, thyme, parsley, grated truffle, and truffle oil until the dough is sticky but smooth.

Coat the colander with nonstick cooking spray. Place the colander over the pot of boiling water, making sure that it sits above the surface of the water. If the bottom of the colander hits the water, ladle some out. Working quickly, with a kitchen mitt or thick dishtowel to protect your hand, hold the colander securely and use a long-handled spoon to press the dough, one-fourth at a time, through the holes, letting the "noodles" drop into the boiling water. When all the dough has been added, cook for 5 minutes, or until the spaetzle float to the top.

Remove the spaetzle with a slotted spoon or mandarin-style strainer to a medium bowl. Toss with the butter.

To serve, place the spaetzle in a large casserole dish and spoon the meatballs and gravy on top. Add fresh thyme sprigs for garnish.

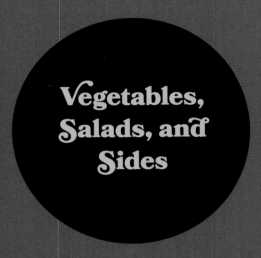

Vegetables, Salads, and Sides

Arrabbiata Spaghetti with Bacon

Bacon-Praline Macaroni and Cheese

Collard Green Dumplings with Red Wasabi Vinaigrette

Boursin Cheese Grits

Loaded Mashed-Potato Cakes

Herb Creamed Mustard Greens

Fresh Kale and Cabbage Slaw

Grandma Lue's Spinach Rice

Spring Pea, Bacon, and Radish Salad

Pimento Cheese, Grits, and Bacon Casserole

Fried Green Tomatoes with Buttermilk Gravy

Okra Succotash

Deviled Egg Po-Boy

Red Bean Risotto with Tasso and Andouille Red-Eye Gravy

Foie Gras Dirty Rice

Collard Green Caesar

Cajun Cornbread Dressing

Cajun Sweet Potato Salad

Garden Vegetable Primavera with Celery Alfredo Sauce

ARRABBIATA SPAGHETTI
With Bacon

SERVES 6 TO 8 AS A SIDE DISH

3 tablespoons kosher salt, divided

1 pound fresh or good-quality dried spaghetti

¼ cup extra-virgin olive oil

3 cloves garlic, smashed

1 onion, chopped

½ cup dry red wine

3 tablespoons tomato paste

1 tablespoon sugar

¼ cup finely chopped fresh basil

1 teaspoon red pepper flakes

1 (28-ounce) can whole San Marzano tomatoes

8 slices bacon, cooked and crumbled

¼ cup finely chopped flat-leaf parsley

This is a great addition to cookouts, and perfect for large gatherings such as reunions or tailgating. Friday was always fish day in our household—and in the Midwest that meant fried fish with spaghetti and coleslaw. The type of fish might change from week to week, but the accompaniments were always the same. My mother's spaghetti was tossed with a flavorful tomato sauce with a hint of spice, much like an Italian Arrabbiata sauce, also know as the "angry" sauce, presumably because of its heat. Add a little bacon (or pancetta) and the dish can easily transform from a side dish to the main attraction. This pasta dish is an incredible partner alongside Blue Cornmeal–Crusted Fried Fish (page 140).

Bring a large pot of water to a boil over high heat. Add 1 tablespoon salt and the spaghetti and cook for 5 to 10 minutes (dried pasta will take longer), until it is just short of al dente. Strain the pasta from the water, reserving 1 cup of water.

Heat the olive oil in a large skillet over medium-high heat. Add the garlic and onion and sauté for 3 to 5 minutes, until translucent. Stir in the wine, tomato paste, remaining 2 tablespoons kosher salt, the sugar, basil, and red pepper flakes. Using your hands, crush the tomatoes as you add them to the skillet. Stir in the reserved pasta water and bring the sauce to a boil, then lower the heat to medium and simmer for 20 minutes. Add the crumbled bacon, parsley, and the cooked pasta and simmer, tossing and stirring often, for another 5 minutes, or until the flavors combine.

BACON-PRALINE MACARONI AND CHEESE

SERVES 12

6 cups elbow macaroni (about 1½ pounds), cooked al dente and drained

1 tablespoon Lawry's Seasoned Salt

1 tablespoon ground white pepper

1 tablespoon garlic powder

1 tablespoon onion powder

3½ cups shredded sharp cheddar cheese (about 1½ pounds), divided

½ cup unsalted butter

½ cup all-purpose flour

8 cups milk, warmed

6 ounces cream cheese, diced

12 ounces American cheese, diced

3 large eggs

8 ounces applewood-smoked bacon (8 to 10 slices), cooked and crumbled

PRALINE TOPPING

½ cup unsalted butter, melted

2 cups coarsely chopped pecans or pecan pieces

1 cup packed light brown sugar

½ cup dried breadcrumbs

James Hemings, the chef and slave of Thomas Jefferson, is credited for introducing the nation to what we call macaroni and cheese. Originally it was considered a refined, upper-crust dish with roots stretching back to Italy, France, and England. As the dish gained popularity and its ingredients became more accessible to the average person, it became more of a comfort food for the masses, rather than a dish reserved for the rich.

For me, its roots trace back to the sixties when commodity food, which included processed cheese, was distributed by the government to tables like mine. Although I have tasted versions of this dish all over the world, with cheeses produce by artisans, it still doesn't compare to ones I've had in the most humble of kitchens. The women of my family were well versed in turning commodity cheese into liquid gold. It was a cheap dish that could feed a lot of people.

This updated version puts a fun twist on a historic dish and is great for serving large groups or for a potluck supper. It can be made days in advance and frozen for convenience. If this recipe is too large, you can freeze half of it for another meal. Just thaw and reheat it in a 325-degree F oven for 20 minutes until heated through. Now that's comfort!

Preheat the oven to 350 degrees F.

Transfer the cooked macaroni to a large bowl.

In a small bowl, stir together the seasoned salt, white pepper, garlic powder, and onion powder. Sprinkle half of this seasoning mixture and 1 cup shredded cheddar cheese over the macaroni and toss to combine.

In a large saucepan over medium-high heat, melt the butter. Whisk in the flour and continue to whisk for 3 to 5 minutes, until it makes a light roux. Reduce the heat to medium and whisk in the milk. Once all the milk is incorporated, cook for another 5 to 8 minutes, until the sauce reaches a simmer. Add the diced cream cheese and American cheese in batches, stirring until smooth. Stir in 1½ cups of the remaining shredded cheddar cheese and turn off the heat. Add the remaining seasoning mixture and stir well. Quickly whisk in the eggs until they are incorporated.

Spread the macaroni mixture evenly into a 12-inch cast-iron skillet. Pour the cheese sauce over the noodles to cover, then fold in the chopped bacon. Top with the remaining 1 cup shredded cheddar cheese. Cover the skillet with foil, transfer to the oven, and bake for 30 minutes, or until the cheese is bubbling around the edges.

FOR THE TOPPING: In a medium bowl, stir all the ingredients together with a fork.

Remove the foil from the baked macaroni and cheese, sprinkle the breadcrumb mixture over the top, and return, uncovered, to the oven. Bake for an additional 15 minutes, or until the topping is golden brown. Let the dish rest for 15 minutes before serving.

COLLARD GREEN DUMPLINGS
With Red Wasabi Vinaigrette

MAKES 40 TO 50 DUMPLINGS

¼ cup extra-virgin olive oil
6 cloves garlic, minced
½ cup finely chopped onion
½ cup finely chopped red bell pepper
¼ cup finely chopped celery
2 pounds fresh collard greens, stemmed, leaves roughly chopped
4 cups chicken broth
1 tablespoon kosher salt
1 teaspoon smoked paprika
1 tablespoon sugar
½ teaspoon red pepper flakes
2 bay leaves
¼ cup apple cider vinegar
½ cup finely chopped scallions
¾ cup cornstarch, for the baking sheet
1 (40- to 50-count) package dumpling or wonton wrappers
2 tablespoons vegetable oil, for pan-frying

RED WASABI VINAIGRETTE
2 teaspoons wasabi powder
½ cup Louisiana-style hot sauce
3 cloves garlic, smashed
¼ cup red wine vinegar
¼ cup chopped flat-leaf parsley
¾ cup extra-virgin olive oil

Both collard greens and dumplings have long been a staple of the soul food community. Typically, our dumplings are just plain dough pieces. When I first tasted Chinese dumplings with their myriad fillings and flavorings, I thought why not try these with collard greens? We eat collards greens with hot sauce and vinegar, too, and that thought was my inspiration for the red wasabi vinaigrette.

These dumplings can be made ahead of time and frozen for up to 3 months. When ready to cook, thaw and proceed with the directions. The red wasabi vinaigrette will last in a lidded container in the refrigerator for 2 weeks.

In a Dutch oven or large heavy-bottomed pot, heat the olive oil over medium-high. Add the garlic, onion, red pepper, and celery, and sauté for 5 minutes, or until the onions are translucent. Add the collard greens and cook for 4 to 5 minutes, stirring, until the greens begin to wilt. Stir in the chicken broth, salt, smoked paprika, sugar, red pepper flakes, bay leaves, and vinegar. Reduce the heat to medium-low and simmer for about 2 hours, until the greens are tender. Remove from the heat and let the collards cool, uncovered, for 30 to 40 minutes, until cool enough to handle.

Strain the liquid from the pot of greens into a bowl and set aside. Using your hands, squeeze any additional liquid out of the collards over the bowl.

Chop the cooked greens into small pieces and transfer to a medium bowl. Stir in the chopped scallions and set aside.

Cover a sheet pan with plastic wrap and dust it with cornstarch. Pour ¾ cup water into a small bowl.

On a clean work surface, lay out 6 dumpling wrappers at a time. Spoon about 2 teaspoons chopped greens into the center of each wrapper. Dip your finger (or a pastry brush) in the water bowl and run it along the edge of half the wrapper to moisten. Fold the wrapper over the filling, creating a half-moon shape, and press the edges firmly together to

seal. Transfer each filled dumpling to the prepared sheet pan, making sure the dumplings don't touch one another (if they do, the wrappers will stick and tear). Repeat until all the dumplings are filled and sealed. At this point, the dumplings can be frozen for up to 3 months (see headnote).

While the greens cool, prepare the vinaigrette. Combine the wasabi powder and 2 teaspoons water in a small (1-cup) food processor and pulse for 1 minute. Add the hot sauce, garlic, vinegar, and parsley and pulse to combine. Slowly drizzle in the olive oil as you process, blending until smooth. Transfer to a bowl and set aside.

In a large skillet, heat 2 tablespoons vegetable oil over medium-high. Working in batches, place a single layer of dumplings in the skillet, being careful not to overcrowd the pan. Add ¼ cup of the reserved collard green liquid and cover the skillet with a lid. Cook for 5 minutes, or until the dumplings are translucent and have browned on the bottom.

With a slotted spoon, transfer the cooked dumplings to a platter, then repeat with the remaining dumplings, adding additional collard green liquid as needed, until all are browned.

Drizzle the vinaigrette over the dumplings before serving them hot or at room temperature. Use any leftover pot liquor as a dipping jus.

BOURSIN CHEESE GRITS

SERVES 6

4 cups milk
1 cup grits
2 tablespoons unsalted butter
1 (5.2-ounce) package Boursin
   Garlic and Fine Herbs
2 ounces cream cheese
1 teaspoon kosher salt
½ teaspoon granulated garlic
½ teaspoon granulated onion
¼ teaspoon ground white
   pepper

Some folks serve grits with sugar or some type of sweetener, which is not my preferred preparation. Savory grits are my thing, and adding cheese makes them perfect as a side dish or as a main course—don't overthink grits. This version, with tangy, easy to find Boursin, is great with any braised meat, rich fish, or stewed poultry.

In a medium saucepan over medium-high heat, bring the milk to a low boil. Whisk in the grits and butter, reduce the heat to medium, and cook for about 15 minutes, whisking occasionally, until the grits begin to soften and absorb the liquid. Whisk in the Boursin, cream cheese, salt, granulated garlic, granulated onion, and white pepper. Reduce the heat to low and cook for 10 to 15 more minutes, stirring occasionally, until the grits are creamy.

Serve with any protein, or the Red-Wine Braised Turkey Necks (page 15).

LOADED MASHED POTATO CAKES

SERVES 6 TO 8

2 cups cold mashed potatoes
¾ cup all-purpose flour
1 cup freshly grated Parmesan
   cheese
6 ounces Andouille or any
   smoked sausage, chopped
¼ cup sundried tomatoes, thinly
   sliced
1 jalapeño, seeded and finely
   diced
2 cloves garlic, minced
5 large eggs, divided
2 teaspoons kosher salt
½ teaspoon ground white
   pepper
½ cup thinly sliced scallions
½ cup milk
1 cup panko-style breadcrumbs
1 teaspoon Lawry's Seasoned
   Salt
1 tablespoon herbes de Provence
¼ cup vegetable oil

I created this recipe for something new to do with a common, and confounding, ingredient we all have on hand at one time or another, leftover mashed potatoes. It has now become one of my favorites because of its versatility. You can use items that are probably already in your cupboard or refrigerator—meats, cheeses, or vegetables. It can be as light or as hearty as you wish, and it's very easy to customize.

These potato cakes can be served as an appetizer, side dish, or a main course with a simple side salad. Try them with Tasso and Andouille Red-Eye Gravy (page 106), Buttermilk Gravy (page 176), or Green Tomato Chimichurri (page 178).

In a large bowl, stir together the mashed potatoes, flour, and Parmesan cheese until combined.

In a medium skillet, brown the sausage over medium-high heat. Add the sundried tomatoes, jalapeño, and garlic and cook, stirring, for 2 to 3 minutes, until heated through. In a small bowl, lightly beat 3 eggs together with a fork.

Transfer the contents of the skillet to the mashed potato mixture, then add the kosher salt, white pepper, scallions, and the beaten eggs and mix thoroughly.

Divide the mixture into 8 equal portions and use your hands to form each into a patty. Transfer the patties to a baking sheet lined with parchment.

In a shallow bowl, mix the remaining 2 eggs and milk with a fork until combined.

In a separate shallow dish, stir together the panko, seasoned salt, and herbes de Provence. Dip each patty in the egg mixture, then dredge in the breadcrumb mixture till well coated. Transfer the breaded potato cakes back to the baking sheet, cover with plastic wrap, and refrigerate for 15 minutes or up to 1 day.

In a medium skillet, heat the oil over medium-high until smoking. Add the chilled potato cakes to the skillet a couple at a time, taking care not to crowd the pan, and pan-fry for 2 to 3 minutes on each side, until golden brown. Transfer to a paper-towel-lined tray to drain.

Serve with your choice of sauce or gravy—or both!

HERB CREAMED MUSTARD GREENS

SERVES 6

2 tablespoons extra-virgin olive oil
1 cup coarsely chopped onion
1 clove garlic, minced
8 cups mustard greens (see headnote), stemmed, leaves chopped into bite-size pieces
2 tablespoons unsalted butter
8 ounces cream cheese, at room temperature
½ cup milk
1 tablespoon chopped chives
½ teaspoon ground nutmeg
1 (5.2-ounce) container Boursin Garlic and Fine Herbs, at room temperature
Salt and freshly cracked black pepper

This is my answer to creamed spinach. Mustard greens are more flavorful than spinach, with a peppery flavor and coarse texture that makes for a tasty spin on a classic dish, but collard or dandelion greens, chard, kale, or a combination would all be delicious. They take a bit longer to cook than spinach, but the extra time is worth it.

In a large skillet, heat the olive oil over medium. Add the onions and garlic and cook, stirring, for 5 to 7 minutes, until the onions are translucent. Stir in the chopped mustard greens and cook for 10 to 12 minutes, until the greens are tender and wilted. Remove from the heat and set aside.

In a heavy saucepan, heat the butter, cream cheese, and milk over medium heat, stirring gently until the cream cheese has melted and the mixture is smooth. Reduce the heat to low and stir in the chives and nutmeg. Add the Boursin and stir until smooth. Season with salt and pepper to taste, then add the cheese mixture to the skillet of cooked greens. Warm through over medium heat and serve immediately.

FRESH KALE AND CABBAGE SLAW

SERVES 6

2 cups thinly sliced kale leaves

2 cups thinly sliced cabbage
  leaves

¼ cup thinly sliced sweet onion,
  such as Vidalia

½ cup shredded carrots

½ cup thinly sliced red bell
  pepper

VINAIGRETTE

⅓ cup apple cider vinegar

¼ cup honey (see headnote)

1 tablespoon Dijon mustard

1 tablespoon garlic powder

1 tablespoon onion powder

1 tablespoon kosher salt

½ teaspoon ground white
  pepper

½ cup extra-virgin olive oil

This dish is light and simple and goes with any meat, poultry, or seafood. I use it in spring rolls and as a topping on tacos, as a condiment on sandwiches, as well as for a side dish. It's both dairy and gluten free—and if you use agave instead of honey, vegan-friendly. Add your own twist by tossing in nuts, berries, or dried fruit. It's an all-around people-pleasing salad to bring to a cookout, pair with the Baby Back Ribs with Sweet Tea Barbecue Sauce (page 38), or serve with the Blue Cornmeal– Crusted Fried Fish (page 140) and Arrabbiata Spaghetti with Bacon (page 83) on Fridays.

In a large bowl, toss the kale, cabbage, onions, carrots, and red peppers.

MAKE THE VINAIGRETTE: In a separate bowl, or a blender, mix together the vinegar, ½ cup water, the honey, mustard, garlic powder, onion powder, salt, and white pepper. Slowly drizzle in the olive oil, blending to emulsify the vinaigrette.

Dress the kale and cabbage mixture with the vinaigrette, toss well, and refrigerate for at least 30 minutes or up to 24 hours, so the dressing can season and tenderize the slaw.

GRANDMA LUE'S SPINACH RICE

SERVES 6 TO 8

3 cups cooked white rice, chilled
2 large eggs, beaten
½ cup (1 stick) unsalted butter
½ cup chopped celery
½ cup chopped red bell pepper
1 cup chopped red onion
4 pounds fresh baby spinach, washed and trimmed
1 cup chopped marinated artichokes
12 ounces cream cheese, at room temperature
½ cup sour cream
1 cup grated Parmesan cheese
2 cloves garlic, minced
½ teaspoon freshly cracked black pepper
½ teaspoon onion powder
½ teaspoon garlic powder
1 teaspoon kosher salt

This delicious rice is named after my grandmother because she devised it as a way to make me eat spinach, and it worked! I added some of my favorite flavors—vinegary artichokes, the combination of cheeses—until the result becomes like the best spinach and artichoke dip you ever had, but with rice, and I love anything with rice.

Preheat the oven to 350 degrees F. Generously grease a deep casserole or 13 x 9-inch baking pan.

In a large bowl, stir together the cold rice and beaten eggs.

In a large skillet over medium-high heat, melt the butter. Add the celery, peppers, onions, and spinach and cook, stirring occasionally, for 2 to 3 minutes, until the onions are translucent and the spinach is wilted. Reduce the heat to medium and stir in the artichokes, cream cheese, sour cream, Parmesan, and garlic. Cook for 5 to 7 minutes, stirring occasionally, until the cream cheese has melted and all of the ingredients are well combined.

Add the spinach-cheese mixture to the rice. With a wooden spoon, stir in the black pepper, onion powder, garlic powder, and salt.

Pour into the prepared casserole, and cover with foil. Bake for 20 minutes, then remove the foil and bake for an additional 10 minutes, or until the top is nicely browned. Let rest for 15 minutes before serving.

SPRING PEA, BACON, AND RADISH SALAD

SERVES 6

3 cups fresh or frozen peas (thawed, if frozen), blanched and drained, then chilled

6 slices applewood smoked bacon, cooked and crumbled

1 cup thinly sliced radishes

½ cup chopped red onion

¼ cup chopped fresh mint, plus additional leaves for garnish

1 teaspoon lemon zest

2 to 3 tablespoons mayonnaise

1 tablespoon honey

Salt and ground white pepper

This is a pretty spring salad in which you can use either fresh or frozen, thawed peas (canned green peas are better left to distant childhood memories, or at least not salads). Fresh mint brightens all of the flavors with its spicy-sweet fragrance. Watermelon radishes are my radish of choice for this recipe; they are peppery with a hint of sweetness and add great balance. I love to serve this dish with Salmon Croquettes (page 122) topped with Buttermilk Dressing (page 174).

In a large bowl, combine all the ingredients and toss gently. Garnish with whole mint leaves.

PIMENTO CHEESE, GRITS, AND BACON CASSEROLE

SERVES 8 TO 10

3 cups milk

1¾ cups white quick grits

1 tablespoon kosher salt

2 cups shredded sharp cheddar cheese

8 ounces cream cheese

4 (4-ounce) jars diced pimentos, drained

1 tablespoon garlic powder

1 tablespoon onion powder

¼ teaspoon cayenne pepper

5 dashes Tabasco sauce

1 tablespoon Worcestershire sauce

16 slices applewood smoked bacon, cooked and crumbled

3 scallions, thinly sliced

10 large eggs, beaten well

This marries three great traditions of the South in one delicious dish. It can be made in advance as a main dish for a breakfast or brunch. It's a twist on the traditional grits casserole, with the spicy pimento cheese adding a knockout punch.

Preheat the oven to 350 degrees F. Generously grease a 9 x 13-inch baking dish with cooking spray.

In a large saucepan, bring 5 cups water and the milk to a boil over medium-high heat. Whisk in the grits a small amount at a time to prevent lumps. Add the salt and reduce the heat to low. Cook the grits for about 20 minutes, whisking frequently, until they are soft and creamy.

Remove the saucepan from the heat and whisk in the cheddar cheese, cream cheese, pimentos, garlic powder, onion powder, cayenne, Tabasco, and Worcestershire sauce. Fold in the bacon and scallions. Let cool for 15 minutes, whisking occasionally. Working quickly, whisk in the beaten eggs.

Pour the grits mixture into the prepared baking dish and bake for 40 minutes, or until the casserole is firm to the touch and lightly browned on top. Remove from the oven and let it rest for 20 minutes before serving.

FRIED GREEN TOMATOES
With Buttermilk Gravy

SERVES 8

Buttermilk Gravy (page 176)
4 firm green tomatoes (1½ to 2 pounds)
1 cup all-purpose flour
1 teaspoon kosher salt
¾ cup buttermilk
2 large eggs
1 cup seasoned breadcrumbs
1 teaspoon onion powder
1 teaspoon garlic powder
Vegetable oil, for frying

Historically, the most Southern thing about a fried green tomato is the use of its name in a movie. These tasty treats can be traced to the northern and midwestern United States, as well as to Jewish immigrant communities in the northeast, showing that their well-earned reputation as a comfort food is truly widespread.

Make the gravy; keep warm.

Cut the tomatoes into ½-inch-thick slices.

In a medium bowl, stir together the flour and kosher salt. In another medium bowl, whisk together the buttermilk and eggs until combined. In a shallow dish, stir together the breadcrumbs, onion powder, and garlic powder.

Dredge the tomato slices first in flour, then dip in the buttermilk mixture, and press into the breadcrumbs.

In a cast-iron skillet, heat ½ inch of oil to 350 degrees F over medium. Using tongs, gently transfer the tomato slices, a few at a time, into the hot oil, being careful not to overcrowd the pan. Cook for 2 to 4 minutes on each side, until golden brown. Transfer to a paper-towel-lined plate to drain. Serve immediately with the gravy.

OKRA SUCCOTASH

SERVES 6 TO 8

4 ears fresh sweet corn, shucked

4 sliced applewood smoked bacon

1 large yellow onion, chopped

2 tablespoons minced garlic (2 to 3 cloves)

2 cups fresh okra cut crosswise into ¼-inch-thick slices

2 cups seeded and chopped Roma tomatoes (6 to 8 medium)

1 tablespoon finely diced jalapeño, or to taste

Salt and freshly cracked black pepper

Pinch of sugar

Okra is one of the quintessential vegetables of the South, and one of the most controversial. Arguments regularly ensue on the best ways to cook and serve it: boiled, stewed, in gumbo, fried, dehydrated, or pickled? Regardless of the preparation, okra succotash is a traditional soul food staple. Certain dishes always remind me of home, and this is one I always wanted Mom to make for me when I went home. I love this and will even eat it over rice. One might be tempted to hit the succotash with acid at the end, but I always add a pinch of sugar to bring out the sweetness in dishes full of naturally sweet vegetables such as carrots, sweet peas, and corn. It sounds counterintuitive, but it works!

Use a sharp knife to trim both ends off of the corncobs so they stand flat. In a wide mixing bowl or shallow dish, starting halfway down the cob, cut the kernels from the cob in a smooth downward motion, then flip the cob and repeat on the other half.

In a large skillet over medium-high heat, cook the bacon for 5 to 7 minutes, until browned and crisp. Remove to a paper-towel-lined plate to drain, leaving the fat in the skillet. Reduce the heat to medium and add the onions and garlic.

Cook for 3 to 5 minutes, until the onions are translucent. Add the okra, chopped tomatoes, corn kernels, jalapeño, and salt and pepper to taste. Reduce the heat to low and simmer for 15 minutes, or until the tomatoes soften. Crumble the cooked bacon and stir into the succotash. Taste again, adding more salt and pepper as needed, and finish with a pinch of sugar. Serve as a side dish or over rice.

DEVILED EGG PO-BOY

SERVES 6 (MAKES 3 TO 3½ CUPS SALAD)

12 large eggs, hard-boiled,
   peeled, and coarsely chopped
1 teaspoon Lawry's Seasoned
   Salt
½ teaspoon garlic powder
½ teaspoon onion powder
2 teaspoons white vinegar
¾ cup mayonnaise
1 tablespoon Dijon mustard
3 tablespoons sweet pickle relish
3 tablespoons dill pickle relish
¼ cup diced red bell peppers
¼ cup diced celery
¼ cup chopped yellow onion
3 tablespoons sliced scallions
2 dashes Tabasco sauce
6 Cuban rolls or hoagie buns,
   sliced in half
Sliced tomatoes, for serving
Shredded iceberg lettuce, for
   serving
Dill pickles, for serving

I love this sandwich because it's a cross between deviled eggs and egg salad—and it's easier to make. If you want to add other elements, fried shrimp, oysters, fish, or even fried green tomatoes (page 101) are all at-home on a po-boy. This is a great lunch option throughout the week, as well, since the deviled egg filling will keep in a covered container in the refrigerator for 4 to 5 days.

In a large bowl, stir together the chopped eggs, seasoned salt, garlic powder, and onion powder. Add the vinegar, mayonnaise, mustard, sweet pickle relish, dill pickle relish, red peppers, celery, onions, scallions, and Tabasco and stir until well mixed. Refrigerate for at least 2 hours before serving.

To make the sandwiches, toast the rolls, spread with the deviled egg mixture, and top with sliced tomatoes, shredded iceberg lettuce, and pickles.

RED BEAN RISOTTO
With Tasso and Andouille Red-Eye Gravy

SERVES 10

2 quarts vegetable broth
6 tablespoons olive oil
½ cup medium-diced onion
½ cup medium-diced red bell
  pepper
½ cup chopped celery
3 cloves garlic, minced
2 teaspoons finely chopped
  fresh thyme
2 cups Arborio rice
½ teaspoon cayenne pepper
1 tablespoon Cajun seasoning
1 teaspoon kosher salt
1 tablespoon granulated garlic
1 tablespoon granulated onion
¾ cup dry white wine
2 cups thinly sliced kale leaves
1 pound dried red kidney beans,
  soaked overnight and cooked
  according to package
  directions
½ cup grated Parmesan cheese
¼ cup half-and-half
Salt and ground white pepper

FOR SERVING
1 recipe Tasso Red-Eye Gravy
  (recipe below)
½ cup diced jalapeños (seeded,
  if desired)
2 medium tomatoes, chopped
1 medium onion, diced

TASSO RED-EYE GRAVY
1 cup brewed coffee
2½ cups chicken broth
4 tablespoons unsalted butter
12 ounces tasso ham, diced
12 ounces Andouille or other
  spicy sausage, diced
4 tablespoons all-purpose flour
½ teaspoon kosher salt
½ teaspoon freshly cracked
  black pepper
½ teaspoon garlic powder
½ teaspoon minced fresh thyme

Louisiana meets Italy in this risotto, which is a refinement of a traditional Cajun country dish. Beans are a healthy way to feed a large amount of people inexpensively, at any time of the year—and this impressive dish will really wow your family or guests. The intensely smoky flavor of the tasso and the heat of the Andouille sausage are a great combination, while the white wine and Parmesan combine to yield a richer, creamier texture than traditional red beans and rice. Look for authentic tasso ham online or in specialty meat markets; any spicy sausage can be used in place of the Andouille.

When you are ready to make the risotto, heat the vegetable broth in a medium saucepan over low heat, and keep warm till ready to use.

In a large saucepan, heat the olive oil over medium heat. Add the onion, red pepper, celery, and garlic and cook for about 5 minutes, stirring, until the onion is translucent. Stir in the thyme, rice, cayenne, Cajun seasoning, salt, granulated garlic, and granulated onion and continue to stir for 2 more minutes, or until the rice is well coated with the oil. Immediately add the wine to the skillet and begin adding the warm broth, ½ cup at a time, stirring continuously until the liquid is absorbed. Once the rice has absorbed the first ½ cup of broth, add another, repeating this process ½ cup at a time until about 1 cup of broth remains.

Once most of the broth has been added, fold in the kale and red beans. Stir in the remaining 1 cup broth, then reduce the heat to low, add the Parmesan cheese, half-and-half, and salt and pepper to taste, and continue to cook for 3 to 5 minutes, stirring, until the Parmesan is melted and the risotto rice is tender but not mushy.

Transfer the risotto to a large casserole dish, and ladle the red-eye gravy on top. Pass the garnishes around the table separately.

MAKE THE TASSO RED-EYE GRAVY:
Combine the coffee and chicken broth in a large saucepan and warm over low heat.

In a large skillet, melt the butter over medium heat. Add the diced tasso and Andouille and sauté for about 2 minutes, stirring, until the meat starts to brown. Whisk in the flour and continue to whisk for about 5 minutes, until it loses its raw, white color and begins to turn golden brown. Whisk in the warmed coffee mixture and bring to a simmer, then reduce the heat to medium-low. Simmer for about 15 minutes, whisking occasionally, until the liquid begins to thicken. Stir in the salt, pepper, garlic powder, and thyme and simmer for another 15 minutes to let the flavors meld. Set aside, keeping warm until ready to use.

The gravy can be kept in the refrigerator for up to 5 days, so feel free to make it in advance.

FOIE GRAS DIRTY RICE

SERVES 6 to 8

4 tablespoons duck fat

4 ounces chicken livers, finely chopped

½ cup finely chopped onion

½ cup finely chopped green bell pepper

¼ cup finely chopped red bell pepper

¼ cup finely chopped celery

3 cloves garlic, minced

1½ cups long-grain rice, rinsed to reduce the starch

2 teaspoons Tony Chachere's Original Creole Seasoning

2 teaspoons Louisiana Cajun seasoning, preferably low-sodium

3 cups chicken broth

12 ounces foie gras, chopped

½ cup finely chopped dried apricots

¼ cup chopped flat-leaf parsley

½ cup thinly sliced scallions

I'll admit it, this is definitely a dish designed to impress. The country cooking of the Louisiana bayou meets the delicacy of French cuisine and it's love at first sight. It may sound like an unlikely combination, but dirty rice is traditionally made with chicken livers, so I knew duck livers and foie gras would add an even more luxurious richness. I took it another step by adding sweetness in the form of dried apricots—a classic pairing. To say the impact of this recipe is greater than the sum of its parts would be a delicious understatement.

In a large saucepan, heat the duck fat over medium heat. Add the chicken livers, onion, green and red pepper, celery, and garlic and sauté for 5 to 8 minutes, until the vegetables start to brown. Stir in the rice. Add the Creole seasoning, Cajun seasoning, and chicken broth and stir until combined. Increase the heat to medium-high and bring to a boil, stirring occasionally to prevent the rice from sticking to the bottom of the pan. Reduce the heat to low, cover, and simmer for 15 to 18 minutes, until the liquid is fully absorbed.

Gently fold in the foie gras and apricots. Remove from heat, cover, and let sit for 10 minutes. Transfer the dirty rice to a serving bowl and garnish with the parsley and scallions.

COLLARD GREEN CAESAR

SERVES 10

1 large bunch collard greens,
  stemmed, leaves rolled and
  thinly sliced
3 cloves garlic, minced
1½ teaspoons anchovy paste
3 tablespoons fresh lemon juice
2 teaspoons Dijon mustard
1½ cups mayonnaise
1 teaspoon Tabasco
1 teaspoon Worcestershire
  sauce
1 tablespoon extra-virgin olive oil
1 teaspoon kosher salt
1 teaspoon freshly cracked
  black pepper
¾ cup grated Parmesan cheese
Duck-Fat Grits Croutons (page
  171)
½ cup shaved Parmesan cheese
8 poached eggs, for serving
  (optional)
Smoked Tomato Relish (page
  196)

Although this recipe calls for collard greens, you may substitute kale or mustard greens. There are many small components to this salad, but don't get frustrated by that, as the resulting dish is magnificent. I like to serve this salad with a side of Smoked Tomato Relish (page 196), some shaved Parmesan and I pass additional dressing around the table. The addition of poached eggs makes this gorgeous salad a full main course, and adds to the richness of the dressing.

Place the collard greens in a large salad bowl.

In a blender, combine the garlic, anchovy paste, lemon juice, mustard, mayonnaise, Tabasco, Worcestershire sauce, olive oil, salt and pepper, and Parmesan. Process until smooth; makes about 2 cups dressing.

Just before serving, add ⅓ cup dressing to the salad bowl. Toss gently, making sure to coat the greens thoroughly. Top with the croutons, shaved Parmesan, and poached eggs, if using. Pass the tomato relish and remaining dressing around the table. Leftover dressing can be kept refrigerated in a sealed container for up to 2 weeks.

CAJUN CORNBREAD DRESSING

SERVES 10 to 12

1 pound unsalted butter, plus more for the casserole dish

10 cups day-old cornbread, crumbled into bite-size pieces

2 large yellow onions, finely chopped

6 stalks celery, finely chopped

1 cup finely diced red bell pepper

1 pound Andouille sausage, diced

6 cloves garlic, minced

¼ cup chopped fresh sage

¼ cup chopped fresh thyme

2 tablespoons chopped fresh rosemary

2 tablespoons poultry seasoning

1 cup torn bread or biscuit pieces

9 cups turkey or chicken broth, divided, plus more as needed

½ cup milk

1 tablespoon Lawry's Seasoned Salt

½ tablespoon freshly cracked black pepper

5 large eggs, beaten

I don't use giblets in either stuffing or dressing—a hot take, I know. I prefer to add spicy sausage, and if you like a little heat, you will, too. This is my go-to dressing recipe for any occasion. If preparing this as stuffing for a holiday turkey, set aside one-third before baking, and you'll have enough to serve on the side, too. If you don't have leftovers, make the cornbread from the Cornbread and Pecan Bread Pudding (page 152) at least 1 day before you plan to make the dressing. Leave it out overnight to dry out.

Preheat the oven to 300 degrees F. Butter a large casserole dish.

Spread the cornbread pieces on 2 baking sheets and toast them in the oven on two different racks for 25 to 30 minutes, until the cornbread is crisp and golden. Do not turn the oven off.

In a large skillet or Dutch oven, melt the butter over medium-high heat. Add the onions, celery, and red peppers and sauté for 3 to 5 minutes, until the onions are translucent. Stir in the sausage and cook for an additional 10 minutes, or until browned. Stir in the garlic, sage, thyme, rosemary, and the poultry seasoning, then set the skillet aside to cool.

Increase the oven temperature to 375 degrees F.

In a large mixing bowl, toss the toasted cornbread and torn bread. Scrape in the cooled onion mixture from the skillet, making sure you get all the butter into the bowl; toss thoroughly to combine. Stir half of the broth into the dressing. Add the milk and then stir in the remaining broth a little at a time, until fully absorbed. If the mixture still looks dry, add up to ½ cup broth by the tablespoonful (if the mixture is moist, don't add extra broth). Add the seasoned salt and cracked pepper. Gently stir in the eggs.

Butter a large casserole dish, add the stuffing, cover with foil, and bake for 30 minutes. Rotate the dish and bake for another 30 minutes. Lift the foil and use a meat thermometer to check the temperature in the middle of the dressing; it should be about 155 degrees F. If not, cover and bake for another 10 minutes. Remove the foil and bake for 10 minutes, or until the top is crispy and golden.

CAJUN SWEET POTATO SALAD

SERVES 10

5 cups peeled and cubed sweet
    potatoes (4 to 5 pounds)
¾ cup chopped celery
½ cup chopped red bell pepper
¼ cup chopped scallions
¼ cup chopped red onion
½ cup sweet pickle relish
1 jalapeño, seeded and minced
1 teaspoon Tony Chachere's
    Original Creole Seasoning
1 teaspoon onion powder
1 teaspoon Paul Prudhomme's
    Blackened Seasoning Blend
¾ cup honey, preferably local,
    or agave
3 tablespoons yellow mustard
¼ cup apple cider vinegar
Salt and freshly ground black
    pepper
Crumbled bacon (optional)

The addition of Cajun spices gives a nice, all-important heat to this sweet potato salad. It's not a mayonnaise-based dish, making it picnic-friendly and a hit with my vegan friends as well. Don't tell them I told you about the optional bacon.

Boil the peeled, cubed sweet potatoes for 8 to 10 minutes, until tender but still firm. Drain them, place in a shallow pan, and refrigerate for 20 to 25 minutes, until cooled.

In a large bowl, combine the cooled sweet potatoes, celery, red pepper, scallions, red onions, pickle relish, and jalapeño, and stir gently until well mixed.

In a small bowl, whisk together the Creole seasoning, onion powder, blackened seasoning, honey, mustard, and vinegar until well blended.

Pour the dressing over the sweet potato mixture and gently toss (if the sweet potatoes are starting to fall apart a little, that's all right, as they'll enrich the dressing). Add salt and pepper to taste. If desired, top with crumbled bacon. Serve chilled or at room temperature.

GARDEN VEGETABLE PRIMAVERA

With Celery Alfredo Sauce

SERVES 8

4 cups chopped celery (from 5 or 6 stalks)
¼ cup chopped onion
3 cloves garlic, chopped
3 sprigs fresh thyme
2 cups low-fat milk
1 teaspoon kosher salt, plus more to taste
1 teaspoon ground white pepper
1 tablespoon onion powder
1 pound fettuccine or linguine
½ cup thinly sliced celery
½ cup thinly sliced yellow squash
½ cup thinly sliced zucchini
2 cups broccoli florets
¼ cup sliced leeks (white and light green parts only)
Freshly ground black pepper
Brussels sprouts leaves, for garnish

This light spring or summer dish amazingly doesn't call for heavy cream in the celery Alfredo sauce, which itself is a play on an old Southern recipe made with eggs, called celery cream. In the spirit of creating a lighter, healthier sauce, this recipe uses low-fat milk.

In a medium saucepan, bring 2 quarts of water to a boil. Add the chopped celery, onion, garlic, and thyme. Reduce the heat to low and simmer for 20 minutes, or until the liquid has reduced by half. Strain the vegetables into a bowl, reserving the cooking liquid.

In a food processor, puree the vegetable mixture until it reaches a creamy, smooth consistency, 1 to 2 minutes.

Combine the pureed vegetable mixture, milk, and about half of the reserved liquid in a saucepan. Stir in the salt, white pepper, and onion powder and cook over low heat for 10 to 12 minutes, until thickened. Turn off the heat and cover.

Cook the pasta in a large pot of boiling, salted water until al dente; drain and set aside.

In a large high-sided sauté pan or Dutch oven, stir together the remaining cooking liquid and the sliced celery, yellow squash, zucchini, broccoli, and leeks and cook for about 5 minutes over medium heat, until the vegetables are tender yet firm.

Reduce heat to low, add the vegetable sauce and the cooked pasta to the pan, and toss everything together. Heat over low until warmed through. Season with salt and pepper, garnish with Brussels sprouts leaves, and serve immediately.

Shellfish and Fish

Shrimp and Crab Fritters
with Roasted Garlic and Caramelized Onion Jam

Lobster Beignets with Vanilla Bean Remoulade

Fresh Salmon Croquettes
with Spring Pea, Bacon, and Radish Salad

Gingersnap-Crusted Salmon

Oyster Arancini

Pumpkin Seed–Crusted Trout
with White Lightnin' Butter Sauce

Nola Barbecue Shrimp

Crawfish Gravy
with Scallion, Goat Cheese, and
Black Pepper Biscuits

Curry Catfish Stew

Lobster Etouffée

Paella Macaroni

Blue Cornmeal–Crusted Fried Fish

Crab Loaf

SHRIMP AND CRAB FRITTERS
With Roasted Garlic and Caramelized Onion Jam

MAKES 24 FRITTERS

3 ounces dried rice vermicelli
noodles
1 pound shrimp, minced
1 pound jumbo lump crabmeat,
picked over
1 teaspoon Old Bay Seasoning
¼ teaspoon cayenne pepper
1 teaspoon garlic powder
1 teaspoon onion powder
½ cup chopped red bell pepper
½ cup chopped scallions
3 tablespoons finely chopped
cilantro
3 large eggs, lightly beaten
½ cup grated Parmesan cheese
Vegetable oil, for frying
Roasted Garlic and Caramelized
Onion Jam (page 191), for
serving

Finding (and playing with) the balance between sweet and savory is a consistent theme in traditional soul food cooking. This dish fits that flavor profile perfectly, setting sweet shrimp, crab, and red bell pepper against piquant seasonings and the natural saltiness of Parmesan.

Unlike a typical fritter that uses flour as a binder, this dish gets its structure from rice noodles, cheese, and egg, making for a lighter texture as well as a gluten-free option. These fritters can be made in any size, so they can be served as little appetizers or for an entrée.

The roasted garlic and onion jam contributes another layer of surprising sweetness. It stores well and also makes a great condiment for a cheese platter.

In a large bowl, combine the vermicelli with enough hot water to cover it, and let soak for 10 to 15 minutes, stirring occasionally, until the noodles become soft and pliable. Drain and coarsely chop into 1-inch lengths.

Return the chopped vermicelli to the bowl. Add the remaining ingredients except the vegetable oil and caramelized onion jam and mix well.

Using your hands, lightly form 24 small patties, about 3 to 4 tablespoons each, making sure not to pack tightly; they should be loose and imperfect. Transfer each patty to a parchment-lined baking sheet and refrigerate, uncovered, for 15 minutes.

Preheat the oven to 250 degrees F (or the lowest setting). Line a second baking sheet with paper towels and set aside.

In a large nonstick skillet, heat ¼ inch oil over medium heat until shimmering. Working in batches, add the patties to the skillet and cook for 3 to 4 minutes on each side, until golden brown. Set each fritter on the prepared baking sheet to drain, then transfer to the preheated oven to keep warm while you fry the rest of the fritters, or until ready to serve.

Serve immediately with the garlic and onion jam.

LOBSTER BEIGNETS

With Vanilla Bean Remoulade

MAKES 8 TO 12 APPETIZER SERVINGS

2 pounds large uncooked
    lobster tails (6 to 7 tails) or
    precooked lobster meat
1 teaspoon kosher salt
2 large eggs, beaten
1 scallion, finely chopped
½ cup finely chopped red bell
    pepper
1 tablespoon unsalted butter,
    melted
½ teaspoon Lawry's Seasoned
    Salt
½ teaspoon Old Bay Seasoning
½ teaspoon granulated garlic
½ teaspoon granulated onion
¼ teaspoon cayenne pepper
½ cup all-purpose flour, sifted
Vegetable oil, for frying
Pinch salt
Vanilla Bean Remoulade (page
    188)

This simple, elegant appetizer is spiced to stay true to its Southern roots. It's an excellent option to make for the holidays—lobster is always perfect to serve at any special party. Don't be put off by the idea of using vanilla outside dessert: It has a rich flavor that brings out the natural sweetness of the lobster meat. The remoulade recipe also makes an elegant sauce for the Gingersnap-Crusted Salmon (page 125); if you care to double the recipe, the remoulade will keep for up to 2 weeks in the refrigerator.

If using uncooked lobster tails, fill a large stockpot with 6 inches water and bring to a boil over high heat. Reduce the heat to medium, add the lobster tails and salt, and cook for 3 to 5 minutes, until the shells turn red and the meat becomes opaque white. Remove the tails and transfer them to a bowl of ice water to stop the cooking process. When cool enough to handle, remove the meat from the shells, rinsing away any green tomalley or red row that you find, and chop coarsely. If using precooked lobster meat, proceed with the directions from here.

In a large bowl, combine the chopped lobster meat, eggs, scallion, red pepper, butter, seasoned salt, Old Bay, granulated garlic, granulated onion, and cayenne pepper and mix well. Gradually stir in the flour until a batter forms.

Add 2 inches of oil to a Dutch oven or high-sided heavy skillet, and heat over medium to 375 degrees F. Line a baking sheet with paper towels.

Carefully drop 6 to 8 scoops of batter, about 2 tablespoons each, into the hot oil, being careful not to overcrowd the skillet. Turn once with tongs or a spider, and fry until golden brown on all sides, 3 to 4 minutes total. Transfer to the prepared baking sheet and repeat with the remaining batter to make about 24 beignets in all.

Serve the beignets warm with the remoulade on the side.

FRESH SALMON CROQUETTES
With Spring Pea, Bacon, and Radish Salad

SERVES 6 AS MAIN COURSE, 12 AS HORS D'OEURVES

2 tablespoons unsalted butter
¼ cup diced red onion
¼ cup diced celery
¼ cup diced red bell pepper
2 pounds skinless salmon fillets, coarsely chopped
½ cup Ritz cracker crumbs
1 cup dried breadcrumbs, divided
½ cup mayonnaise
1 tablespoon Dijon mustard
1 tablespoon chopped flat-leaf parsley
1 tablespoon chopped fresh dill
1 tablespoon capers, drained and chopped
2 large eggs, beaten
1 teaspoon Lawry's Seasoned Salt
2 teaspoons granulated onion
2 teaspoons granulated garlic
1 teaspoon Old Bay Seasoning
¼ teaspoon cayenne pepper
¼ cup extra-virgin olive oil
Spring Pea, Bacon, and Radish Salad (page 97)
Buttermilk Dressing (page 174)

My inspiration for this dish is my enduring love for Latin culture and food, specifically Spanish croquetas. Although similar in preparation, they taste entirely different from the salmon croquettes that my grandma made from canned salmon. Of course, the freshness of ingredients is the difference. This recipe uses fresh ingredients, but it is based on my grandma's old recipe—truly the best of both worlds. She served hers with rice and peas, but I pair the croquettes with a fresh pea and radish salad and tangy buttermilk dressing to add lightness and crunchy texture to the meal. These can be made smaller and used as hors d'oeuvres.

Melt the butter in a large skillet over medium heat. Add the onions, celery, and red bell pepper and cook for 3 to 5 minutes, until the onion is translucent. Set aside to cool slightly.

In a large bowl, gently fold together the salmon, cooked vegetables, cracker crumbs, ½ cup of the breadcrumbs, the mayonnaise, mustard, parsley, dill, capers, eggs, seasoned salt, granulated onion, granulated garlic, Old Bay, and cayenne until well combined.

Place the remaining ½ cup breadcrumbs in a shallow bowl.

With your hands, divide the salmon mixture into 6 patties. Dredge each patty in the breadcrumbs, patting to help the crumbs adhere, and transfer to a shallow dish. Cover and refrigerate for 20 minutes to firm.

Preheat the oven to 350 degrees F.

Heat the olive oil in a medium nonstick skillet over medium heat. Add the patties to the skillet and cook for 3 minutes on each side, or until golden brown. Transfer the browned croquettes to a baking dish and bake for 5 to 7 minutes, until firm to the touch.

To serve, divide the pea and radish salad among 6 plates and top each serving with a salmon croquette. Drizzle buttermilk dressing over each croquette, and pass the remaining dressing around the table.

GINGERSNAP-CRUSTED SALMON

SERVES 8

1 cup Soy Vey Veri Veri Teriyaki Marinade and Sauce, or teriyaki sauce of your choice
1 tablespoon peeled and minced fresh ginger
2 tablespoons fresh lemon juice
2 pounds salmon fillet, skin removed, cut into 8 (4-ounce) portions
3 cups crushed gingersnap crumbs (from 30 to 40 cookies)
1 cup panko breadcrumbs
½ cup all-purpose flour
1 teaspoon Chinese five-spice powder
1 teaspoon kosher salt
½ teaspoon ground white pepper
4 large eggs
½ cup milk
6 tablespoons light sesame oil
Vanilla Bean Remoulade (page 188), for serving

I loved gingersnaps as a kid, so when I was thinking of how to get my young daughter to eat salmon, I remembered that salmon pairs well with both sweet and heat. While gingersnaps aren't always sugar-sweet, they have the right bite from the ginger to balance the rich fish. She loved it! Salmon is great to pair with sweet and salty flavors, and the teriyaki marinade adds saltiness, sweetness, and ginger to the taste.

For your convenience, the salmon can be crusted in advance and refrigerated, covered, for 2 days before cooking. This simple preparation is quick and easy for a light dinner or lunch. It's great served with Okra Succotash (page 102) or Fresh Kale and Cabbage Slaw (page 93).

Preheat the oven to 375 degrees F.

In a large shallow dish, combine the teriyaki sauce, fresh ginger, and lemon juice. Add the salmon to the marinade, cover, and let sit for 15 minutes at room temperature, then turn the fillets and marinate on the other side for another 15 minutes. (Do not marinate longer than 30 minutes total.) Remove the fillets and set aside. Discard the marinade.

In another shallow dish, stir together the gingersnap crumbs, panko, flour, five-spice powder, salt, and white pepper.

In a small bowl, whisk together the eggs and milk. Dip each fillet in the egg mixture, then roll in the gingersnap mixture, pressing the crumbs onto the fish. Transfer the fillets to a platter, cover loosely with plastic wrap, and place in the freezer for 15 minutes.

In a large nonstick skillet, heat the sesame oil over medium-high until shimmering. Sear the fillets in the hot oil for 2 to 3 minutes, until browned, then flip and cook on the other side for 2 minutes, or until browned. Using a fish spatula, remove the browned fillets to a baking sheet and transfer to the oven. Bake for 8 to 12 minutes, until the salmon feels firm to the touch.

Serve with a green salad and vanilla bean remoulade.

OYSTER ARANCINI

MAKES ABOUT 24

3 cups low-sodium chicken broth
¾ cup dry white wine
3 tablespoons extra-virgin olive oil
1 onion, finely diced
½ cup finely diced celery
¼ cup finely diced red bell
  pepper
2 cloves garlic, minced
1 cup arborio rice
1 teaspoon lemon zest
1 teaspoon kosher salt
¼ teaspoon cayenne pepper
½ cup shredded Parmesan
  cheese
¼ cup chopped chives
½ cup all-purpose flour
4 large eggs
1½ cups dried Italian
  breadcrumbs
1 pound small oysters (about
  24), shucked
Vegetable oil, for frying
Lemon wedges, for serving
Cocktail sauce, for serving

Arancini are rice balls, usually made with leftover risotto, which get stuffed, breaded, and deep-fried. The traditional Sicilian finger food can be stuffed with ragù, mozzarella, ham, or peas. I chose to use oysters and a little spice to give it a Creole spin. What makes this dish perfect for entertaining is that the risotto balls can be made several days ahead and refrigerated. All you need do is quickly fry them up and serve hot for an irresistible almost impromptu appetizer.

In a medium saucepan, warm the chicken broth and wine over low heat.

In a large saucepan, heat the olive oil over medium, then add the onion, celery, red pepper, and garlic and sauté for 2 minutes, or until the onion is translucent. Add the rice and stir constantly with a wooden spoon for 3 to 5 minutes, until the rice is well coated and begins to brown slightly.

Add ½ cup warmed broth and stir until the liquid is fully absorbed by the rice. Continue with the rest of the broth, ½ cup at a time, stirring the mixture until each addition is completely integrated before adding the next. Once all of the broth has been added, continue to cook for 15 to 20 more minutes, stirring occasionally, until the risotto is tender and creamy. Off the heat, stir in the lemon zest, salt, cayenne, Parmesan cheese, and chives until well blended.

Spread the risotto on a sheet pan and refrigerate for at least 20 minutes to cool, or if you plan to make the arancini the next day, cover the risotto with plastic wrap and keep refrigerated until you are ready to finish the recipe.

Put the flour in a shallow bowl or baking dish. Beat the eggs together in a medium bowl. Place the breadcrumbs in a third bowl or baking dish.

Line a baking sheet with parchment. Scoop a heaping tablespoon of the chilled risotto into your hand, enough to cover an entire oyster. Insert 1 oyster into the center of the risotto, gently close the rice around it, and use your hands to roll it into a smooth round ball. Next, roll the ball in the flour, then the egg, then through the breadcrumbs until well coated. Transfer each ball to the lined baking sheet. Repeat the process until all of the oysters are rolled in risotto and coated. Transfer the baking sheet to the refrigerator while you heat the oil for frying. Or, if you prefer, the arancini will keep, covered, in the refrigerator for 2 to 3 days.

Line another baking sheet with paper towels.

In a Dutch oven or deep heavy saucepan, bring 4 inches of vegetable oil to 350 degrees F over medium-high heat. One at a time, carefully add the risotto balls to the hot oil, being careful not to overcrowd the pot. Fry the arancini for about 5 minutes, turning with tongs or a spider, until golden brown and crispy. With a slotted spoon, transfer the arancini to the prepared baking sheet to drain. Repeat until all are fried.

Serve warm or at room temperature with lemon wedges and your favorite cocktail sauce.

PUMPKIN SEED–CRUSTED TROUT

With White Lightnin' Butter Sauce

SERVES 8

8 (6-ounce) skin-on trout fillets
2 teaspoons kosher salt, divided
1 teaspoon freshly cracked black
  pepper
1 teaspoon onion powder
1 teaspoon garlic powder
1½ cups shelled raw pumpkin
  seeds
1 cup all-purpose flour
3 large eggs
¼ cup vegetable oil
4 tablespoons unsalted butter
White Lightnin' Butter Sauce
  (page 177), warmed, for serving

I came up with this recipe as a way to get rid of pumpkin seeds left over from Halloween. Rainbow trout is a fairly mild-flavored fish. The pumpkin seeds add texture and richness to the fish, and the butter sauce makes it special. It's a great fall dinner and a quick, impressive meal for company. Although white lightning moonshine has a checkered history and was the illegal drink of choice of many of my ancestors, high-quality commercial versions can now be purchased legally at most liquor outlets. As the inspiration for this dish, it gives a more intense flavor than wine or other spirits.

Prepare the white lightning butter sauce and set aside to keep warm.

On a baking sheet, season the fillets with 1 teaspoon kosher salt.

In a food processor, pulse the remaining 1 teaspoon salt, black pepper, onion powder, garlic powder, pumpkin seeds, and flour until the seeds are finely chopped, about 6 to 8 pulses. Do not over-process or you'll get pumpkin seed butter. Transfer the mixture to a shallow dish.

In another shallow bowl, whisk together the eggs and milk. Dip each fillet in the egg mixture to coat, then roll in the pumpkin seed mixture, pressing firmly until each fillet is well coated. Return the fillets to the baking sheet, cover loosely with plastic wrap, and refrigerate for at least 30 minutes.

When ready to pan-fry the fish, line another baking sheet with paper towels.

Combine the vegetable oil and butter in a large nonstick skillet over medium-high heat. Once hot, add half of the fillets skin-side down and cook for 3 to 4 minutes, then turn and cook for another 3 to 4 minutes, until golden brown on both sides. Transfer to the paper-towel-lined baking sheet to drain. Repeat with the remaining fillets.

Drizzle with the warmed butter sauce and serve immediately.

NOLA BARBECUE SHRIMP

SERVES 6 TO 8

4 sticks (1 pound) unsalted butter
¼ cup extra-virgin olive oil
1 shallot, minced
8 cloves garlic, minced
½ cup Worcestershire sauce
1 teaspoon finely chopped fresh thyme
1 teaspoon finely chopped fresh oregano
1 teaspoon finely chopped flat-leaf parsley
2 tablespoons fresh lemon juice
½ teaspoon cayenne pepper
1 tablespoon paprika
1 tablespoon Tony Chachere's Original Creole Seasoning
3 bay leaves
3 pounds (18 to 20 count) jumbo shrimp, heads-on

Growing up with a Louisiana-born grandfather had its advantages at dinnertime. He made the best gumbos, boudin sausage, and fried fish in the entire world. To this day, whatever ability I have to cook up some incredible Louisiana Cajun fare, I credit to his influence. One dish I favor in particular is NOLA (as in, New Orleans, Louisiana) barbecue shrimp. I'll whip this up at the drop of a hat when I'm hungry and want a little spice in my life. It's rich and decadent, but simple to make. The shrimp can be prepared with the shell off, but I prefer to leave both the head and shell on to seal in the shrimp's delicate flavor. It's messy, yes, but worth it!

I serve these shrimp with crusty bread or Scallion, Goat Cheese, and Black Pepper Biscuits (page 133) so I can sop up every drop of the sauce.

Preheat the oven to 350 degrees F.

In a large skillet, melt the butter over medium heat, stir in the olive oil, and add the shallot and minced garlic. Sauté for 2 minutes, or until the shallot is translucent and the garlic turns golden. Whisk in the Worcestershire sauce, thyme, oregano, parsley, lemon juice, cayenne, paprika, and Creole seasoning. Reduce the heat to low and simmer for 10 minutes to let the flavors meld. Add the bay leaves and continue to simmer for another 15 minutes.

Place the shrimp in a 9 by 13-inch baking dish, pour the sauce over the shrimp, and bake for 10 minutes. Flip the shrimp, stir, and bake for another 5 minutes to infuse the flavor of the sauce into the whole shrimp. Remove from the oven and let sit for 5 minutes.

Serve with a sliced baguette or biscuits.

CRAWFISH GRAVY
With Scallion, Goat Cheese, and Black Pepper Biscuits

SERVES 6 to 8

BISCUITS
4 cups all-purpose flour
4 teaspoons baking powder
1 teaspoon baking soda
1½ teaspoons kosher salt
2 teaspoons freshly cracked
   black pepper
¾ cup crumbled goat cheese
   (8 to 10 ounces)
¼ cup thinly sliced scallions
¾ cup (1½ sticks) unsalted
   butter, frozen
1¾ cups buttermilk

CRAWFISH GRAVY
2 tablespoons vegetable oil
4 tablespoons unsalted butter
6 tablespoons all-purpose
   flour
1 medium onion, finely diced
2 cloves garlic, minced
½ cup finely diced green bell
   pepper
¼ cup finely diced celery
¼ cup finely diced red bell
   pepper
1 teaspoon Old Bay Seasoning
1 teaspoon Tony Chachere's
   Original Creole Seasoning
1 teaspoon paprika
1 tablespoon liquid crab boil
   (see headnote)
2 cups seafood stock or
   chicken broth, at room
   temperature
2 pounds crawfish tail meat,
   picked over
½ cup heavy cream
3 tablespoons dry sherry

At any gathering of my Louisiana family, crawfish gravy would be passed around the table along with the grits, eggs, white rice, or biscuits. Sometimes referred to as the "poor man's lobster," crawfish is and always will be included in my food memories of what makes Louisiana special. It tastes similar to lobster, and lends itself to many preparations. I have served it with poached eggs and biscuits for brunch, and with a nice salad for dinner. Look for liquid crab boil in the seafood section of the supermarket.

Homemade biscuits are the love that belongs on every table. Through the years I've discovered many combinations of ingredients to enhance my biscuit repertoire; this recipe is one of my favorites. The combination of savory flavors balances well with almost any dish. These biscuits go well with most any compound butter (see page 172), jam, or gravy.

MAKE THE BISCUITS: Preheat the oven to 425 degrees F.

In a large bowl, stir together the flour, baking powder, baking soda, salt, black pepper, then add the goat cheese, and scallions. Form a well in the center, grate in the frozen butter using the large holes of a cheese grater, and cut the butter into the flour mixture with a fork or pastry cutter. Stir in the buttermilk, a little at a time, until it just comes together, then use your hands to knead the mixture into a soft dough. Be careful not to overmix or the biscuits will be dense.

Turn the dough out onto a lightly floured work surface. Flour a rolling pin and roll the dough out into a large rectangle about 1 inch thick. Cut out the biscuits using a 2-inch-round biscuit cutter and transfer them to a baking sheet, leaving some space around each biscuit. Cover with plastic wrap and chill in the freezer for 15 minutes.

Bake for 15 to 20 minutes, until the biscuits are tall and lightly golden brown. Let cool slightly on a wire rack for 15 minutes while starting the gravy.

MAKE THE GRAVY: In a Dutch oven or cast-iron skillet, heat the vegetable oil and butter over medium heat until the butter is melted. Whisk in the flour, reduce the heat to low, and cook, whisking constantly, until the roux turns a caramel color, 4 to 5 minutes. Add the onion, garlic, green pepper, celery, and red pepper, and sauté, stirring frequently, for 15 minutes, or until the vegetables are soft. Stir in the Old Bay, Creole seasoning, paprika, crab boil, and seafood stock. Increase the heat to medium-high, bring to a simmer, and cook for 25 minutes, or until the mixture begins to thicken. Stir in the crawfish and heavy cream and simmer for another 5 minutes, or until the crawfish is just cooked through. Finish with the sherry, cover, and let sit for 5 minutes before serving.

Serve the gravy hot over the biscuits; it also goes well with white rice or creamy grits. Leftover gravy can be kept in an airtight container in the refrigerator for up to 3 days, and reheated on the stovetop or in a microwave.

CURRY CATFISH STEW

SERVES 8

3 tablespoons vegetable oil

1 onion, chopped

1 red bell pepper, chopped

1 green bell pepper, chopped

1 cup chopped celery

3 scallions, thinly sliced

4 cloves garlic, minced

3 tablespoons finely chopped fresh ginger

2 lemongrass stalks, outer parts removed, tender inner parts finely chopped

2 jalapeños, seeded and thinly sliced

3 tablespoons hot curry powder

1 teaspoon ground coriander

1 teaspoon ground cumin

2 tablespoons kosher salt

2 teaspoons freshly cracked black pepper

2 tablespoons granulated garlic

2 tablespoons granulated onion

2 (13.5-ounce) cans coconut milk

6 cups chicken broth

2 medium potatoes, peeled and diced (about 2 cups)

4 medium carrots, sliced ½ inch thick (about 2 cups)

2 cups peeled and diced butternut squash

1 bunch mustard greens, stemmed and thinly sliced (about 4 cups, packed)

3 tablespoons cornstarch

2 pounds catfish fillets, cut into 1- to 1½-inch pieces

¼ cup chopped cilantro

This hearty stew is a melting pot of flavors. I picked spices from all over the globe— the recipe is a blend of flavors from Asia, India, and Jamaica, each home to delicious curries, with a little touch of Mexico—and the catfish and mustard greens come from soul food traditions. It's a strength-in-diversity stew!

In a large Dutch oven or heavy-bottomed pot, heat the oil over medium. Add the onion, red pepper, green pepper, celery, scallions, garlic, ginger, lemongrass, and jalapeños. Stir the vegetables and sauté for 3 to 5 minutes, until softened.

Stir in the curry powder, coriander, cumin, salt, black pepper, granulated garlic, and granulated onion. Add the coconut milk and chicken broth and simmer for 10 minutes. Reduce the heat to low and add the potatoes, carrots, squash, and mustard greens. Cover and simmer for 10 to 15 minutes, stirring occasionally to prevent sticking, until the potatoes and squash are just cooked but still firm.

In a small bowl, stir together cornstarch and 3 tablespoons cold water to make a quick slurry to help thicken the sauce and give it body. Whisk the slurry into the pot.

Stir in the catfish pieces and cilantro, cover, and continue to cook for another 10 to 15 minutes, until the fish flakes easily.

Off the heat, remove the cover, and let the stew sit for 10 minutes to allow the flavors to meld.

Serve with a sliced baguette or crusty bread.

LOBSTER ETOUFFÉE

SERVES 6

4 (4- to 5-ounce) uncooked
   lobster tails
3 bay leaves, divided
1 cup chopped yellow onion,
   peels and scraps reserved
1 shallot, chopped, peels and
   scraps reserved
1 cup chopped celery, peels and
   scraps reserved
¾ cup chopped green bell
   pepper, peels and scraps
   reserved
6 frozen vol au vent or puff
   pastry shells, thawed
¼ cup vegetable oil
4 tablespoons unsalted butter
½ cup all-purpose flour
4 cloves garlic, minced
1 teaspoon Old Bay Seasoning
2 teaspoons kosher salt
1 teaspoon liquid crab boil (see
   page 133)
1 (14.5-ounce) can Ro-Tel
   tomatoes, with juice
1 pinch of cayenne pepper

Etoufée is a classic Cajun or Creole smothered stew made with shellfish and vegetables, traditionally served over rice. Every time I encounter the telltale fragrance of this dish—the singular scent of a dark brown roux—I'm reminded of home, and I can feel that impatient sense of anticipation for something good on its way begin to grow, knowing that gravy will be on the table soon.

Instead of serving this etouffée over rice, as is customary, I have chosen to use a buttery puff pastry (basically fancy biscuits!) to showcase the lobster and gravy.

Using a sharp knife, split the lobster tails in half, remove the meat, and cut into ¾- to 1-inch pieces, reserving the shells. Transfer the meat to a medium bowl, cover, and refrigerate while preparing the lobster stock.

In a medium saucepan, combine 4 cups water, the lobster shells, 1 bay leaf, and the peels and scraps from the onion, shallot, celery, and green pepper and bring to a boil over medium-high heat. Reduce the heat to medium and simmer for 30 to 40 minutes, until the stock has reduced by half. Strain, reserving the stock and discarding the shells. Set the stock aside.

While the stock is reducing, prepare the puff pastry shells according to the package instructions. Set aside.

In a medium cast-iron skillet, heat the oil and butter over medium until the butter melts. Whisk in the flour, reduce the heat to low, and cook for 6 to 8 minutes, whisking constantly, until the roux turns a dark caramel color. Stir in the onion, shallot, garlic, celery, and green pepper and sauté for about 15 minutes, stirring frequently, until the vegetables start to brown.

Add the Old Bay, salt, crab boil, tomatoes, remaining 2 bay leaves, 1 cup water, and the reserved lobster stock. Increase the heat to medium-high and simmer, stirring frequently, for 25 minutes, or until the stew thickens. Off the heat, gently fold in the lobster pieces and cover. Let sit for 10 minutes, then sprinkle with the cayenne pepper.

To serve, spoon the etouffée into and over the puff pastry shells.

PAELLA MACARONI

SERVES 8 TO 10

¼ cup extra-virgin olive oil
1 onion, chopped
1 red bell pepper, finely chopped
1 green bell pepper, finely
  chopped
6 cloves garlic, finely chopped
1 pound boneless, skinless
  chicken thighs (about 4), cut
  into 1-inch pieces
1 cup thinly sliced chorizo,
  Andouille, or any spicy, cured
  sausage
1 cup white wine
3 cups chicken broth
1 tablespoon kosher salt
1 teaspoon ground white pepper
1 tablespoon granulated garlic
1 tablespoon granulated onion
2 teaspoons paprika
2 teaspoons saffron threads
1 pound elbow macaroni
16 mussels, de-bearded, rinsed,
  and scrubbed
16 clams, rinsed and scrubbed
4 ounces frozen calamari rings,
  thawed
1 pound (21 to 25 count) large
  shrimp, peeled and deveined
12 to 15 ounces lobster meat
  (picked from 3 large tails),
  chopped
½ cup frozen peas
3 tablespoons finely chopped
  flat-leaf parsley
Lemon wedges, for serving

This paella really initiated my thinking about the similarities in comfort foods around the world. I tasted it in Lugo, Spain, at a friend of a friend's house for dinner. They served paella, but made it with macaroni noodles instead of rice. Although I'd eaten traditional Spanish paella many times, this version really stood out to me. I liked the creamier texture of the saffron sauce mixed with the starch of the macaroni. I think it's even more flavorful than the traditional version and makes an especially striking presentation for parties.

In a paella pan or extra-large skillet (preferably cast-iron), heat the oil over medium-high. Add the onion, red pepper, green pepper, and garlic and cook for 3 to 5 minutes, until the onion is translucent.

Add the chicken and sauté for 10 to 12 minutes, until the chicken is lightly browned. Stir in the chorizo, white wine, chicken broth, salt, white pepper, granulated garlic powder, granulated onion, paprika, and saffron threads.

Bring to a boil, then stir in the macaroni. Reduce the heat to medium and cook for 5 minutes. Stir in the mussels, clams, and calamari, cover, and cook for 5 more minutes. Add the shrimp, lobster,

and green peas, cover, and cook for another 5 minutes, or until the shellfish and peas have just cooked through and are still brightly colored.

Remove the pan from the heat and let the paella rest, covered, for 10 minutes. Remove the cover and stir. Discard any mussels or clams that are not open.

Garnish with the parsley and serve with lemon wedges.

BLUE CORNMEAL–CRUSTED FRIED FISH

SERVES 6

1 teaspoon onion powder
1 teaspoon garlic powder
1 teaspoon Lawry's Seasoned
  Salt
½ teaspoon cayenne pepper
6 (16- to 18-ounce) whole red
  snappers, cleaned
2 large eggs, beaten
½ cup milk
2 cups finely ground blue
  cornmeal
1 teaspoon kosher salt
Vegetable oil, for frying

Fried fish was served every Friday in our home and that is a tradition that I still follow to this day. Either we would cook it at home, buy it and have it cooked at the fish market, or run by and purchase it at a local church fish fry. Fish fries are a popular communal event that started during slavery and became a tradition that migrated with African Americans throughout the country. Regionally, you will find different side dishes offered up with the fish—from grits to fries to hush puppies—but, since I'm from the Midwest, it's spaghetti. I love to pair this snapper with Arrabbiata Spaghetti with Bacon for cookouts, reunions, or a special Friday dinner.

In a small bowl, stir together the onion powder, garlic powder, seasoned salt, and cayenne.

Rinse the fish under cold running water and pat dry with paper towels. On a platter or baking sheet, sprinkle both sides generously with the seasoning mixture. Cover loosely with plastic wrap and refrigerate for 30 minutes.

In a shallow dish, whisk together the eggs and milk. In another shallow dish, stir together the cornmeal and salt.

Dip each fillet in the egg mixture, then roll both sides in the cornmeal to coat.

Line a tray or sheet pan with paper towels.

In a Dutch oven or cast-iron skillet, heat 1½ inches of oil over medium-high. When the oil reaches 350 degrees F, add the fish, two at a time, and fry for 5 to 7 minutes on each side, until they are crisp and golden brown. Some pieces may take longer depending on thickness. Use a slotted spoon to transfer the fish to the prepared baking sheet to drain. Note: Since you are cooking 3 batches, monitor the heat so that the oil continues to bubble but doesn't burn.

Serve immediately with Arrabbiata Spaghetti with Bacon (page 183).

CRAB LOAF

SERVES 12

2 pounds fresh jumbo lump
  crabmeat, thoroughly picked
3 tablespoons unsalted butter
½ cup finely diced onion
½ cup finely diced celery
½ cup finely diced red bell pepper
¼ cup finely diced green bell
  pepper
3 large eggs, lightly beaten
2 teaspoons Old Bay Seasoning
½ teaspoon dry mustard
¼ teaspoon cayenne pepper
1 cup dried Italian breadcrumbs
2 tablespoons thinly sliced
  scallions, for garnish
White Lightnin' Butter Sauce
  (page 177), for serving

This dish is a cross between a crab cake and a meatloaf. I like to use it as a starter, served over a bed of arugula and drizzled with White Lightnin' Butter Sauce.

Preheat the oven to 350 degrees F.

Place the crabmeat in a large bowl. With your fingers, make sure the crabmeat has been thoroughly picked clean of any bits of shell.

In a medium skillet, melt the butter over medium heat. Add the onion, celery, red pepper, and green pepper and sauté for 3 to 5 minutes, until the onion is translucent. Remove from the heat and set aside to cool.

Once cool, stir the vegetable mixture into the crabmeat. Add the eggs, Old Bay, mustard, cayenne, and bread-crumbs and mix until well combined.

Turn the mixture into a lightly greased 5 by 9-inch loaf pan and bake for 40 to 50 minutes, until the loaf is firm to the touch and the top is slightly browned.

Let the loaf cool for 15 to 20 minutes before serving with the butter sauce. Garnish with the scallions.

Desserts

Fried Apple Hand Pies with Milk Jam

Strawberry Moonshine Pound Cake
with Moscato Sabayon

Cornbread and Pecan Bread Pudding
with Bourbon-Bacon Glaze

Navy Bean Pie

Lemon Blueberry Buckle

Red Velvet Crème Brûlée
with Vanilla Bean Cream Cheese Frosting

Benne Seed Wafers with Chocolate Gravy

Chocolate Buttermilk Pie

Aunt Lucille's 7-Up Pound Cake

Bananas Foster Banana Pudding

FRIED APPLE HAND PIES
With Milk Jam

MAKES 8 TO 10 PIES

MILK JAM
3 (12-ounce) cans evaporated milk
1½ cups granulated sugar
½ teaspoon baking soda
½ vanilla bean, split lengthwise and seeds scraped (reserve the bean)

PASTRY
2 cups all-purpose flour
1 teaspoon salt
½ cup shortening, refrigerated for 30 minutes

APPLE FILLING
3 Granny Smith apples, peeled and cut into medium dice
1 tablespoon fresh lemon juice
2 tablespoons unsalted butter
⅓ cup packed brown sugar
¼ teaspoon ground cinnamon
¼ teaspoon ground cardamom
1 pinch of ground ginger
¼ teaspoon lemon zest
¼ teaspoon orange zest
Vegetable oil, for frying

Milk jam is made all over the world with different names, and it differs from one country to the other. This Southern version is richer and thicker than a caramel, with an intense sugar-cream sweetness. If you don't have an electric fryer with a thermometer, use a candy or deep-fry thermometer to measure the temperature of the oil. Two pieces of advice: Make sure you cook the pies only 2½ minutes on each side, because these pastries can burn easily. And don't overcrowd the skillet—that lowers to temperature of the oil and make it be harder to handle the pies when turning.

MAKE THE MILK JAM: In a large heavy saucepan over medium heat, stir together the evaporated milk, sugar, and baking soda, and cook for 10 minutes to jumpstart the caramelization. Add the vanilla seeds and the split bean, and stir to dissolve. Once the sugar has dissolved, reduce the heat to low. Cook for another 2½ to 3 hours, stirring occasionally, until the mixture darkens to a golden brown and has reduced to about 1¼ cups. Don't worry if there is some separation.

Strain the mixture through a fine-mesh strainer. Use immediately, or let the jam cool completely, transfer to a sealed container, and refrigerate for 7 to 10 days.

MAKE THE PASTRY: In a medium bowl, blend the flour and salt together. Use a fork to cut in the shortening until the mixture resembles coarse crumbs. Add 1½ cups ice water, a little at a time, mixing with a fork until the dough is just moistened and holds together.

Divide the dough in half and make two 1-inch-thick discs (about 8 inches in diameter). Wrap each disc with plastic wrap and refrigerate for 30 minutes or up to 5 days.

WHILE THE DOUGH IS CHILLING, MAKE THE APPLE FILLING: Toss the diced apples with the lemon juice in a medium bowl.

Melt the butter in a saucepan over medium-low heat. Add the apples, brown sugar, cinnamon, cardamom, ginger, lemon zest, and orange zest and stir until the apples are well coated. Increase the heat to medium and cook for 10 to 12 minutes, until the apples begin to soften. Set aside to cool.

Transfer the chilled dough to a lightly floured work surface, and roll one disc out to a ⅛-inch thickness. Using a 6-inch-diameter circle cookie cutter, cut out three to four rounds, gathering up any scraps, rolling them out once again, and cutting out more 6-inch rounds. Repeat with the second disc. You should have a total of 8 to 10 rounds.

Place 1 tablespoon of the apple mixture a little off the center on each round. Moisten the edges with water, fold the pastry in half over the apple filling, and seal by pressing down gently along the dough edge with a fork.

In a large skillet, heat 1 inch of oil to 375 degrees F, and fry the pies, a few at a time, for 2½ minutes on each side, or until they are light golden brown. With a slotted spoon, transfer the fried pies to paper towels to drain and let cool slightly.

To serve, top each pie with a spoonful of warm milk jam.

Fried pies can be frozen for up to 1 month. Reheat the pies in a preheated 375-degree F oven for 5 to 7 minutes.

STRAWBERRY MOONSHINE POUND CAKE *With Moscato Sabayon*

SERVES 10 TO 12

POUND CAKE

1 cup (2 sticks) unsalted butter, at room temperature, plus more for the pan

3 cups all-purpose flour, sifted, plus a little for the pan

2 cups chopped fresh or frozen strawberries

2¼ cups granulated sugar, divided

½ cup White Lightnin' Moonshine (or other clear moonshine), divided

1 teaspoon baking soda

½ teaspoon baking powder

½ teaspoon salt

1 teaspoon vanilla extract

1 teaspoon almond extract

4 large eggs

⅔ cup buttermilk

3 tablespoons finely chopped fresh basil

GLAZE

1½ cups chopped fresh strawberries

½ cup granulated sugar

1 tablespoon cornstarch

Strawberry moonshine (reserved from soaking the strawberries)

¼ cup confectioners' sugar

MOSCATO SABAYON

4 large egg yolks

¼ cup granulated sugar

½ cup Moscato, or another sweet dessert wine

1 teaspoon fresh lemon juice

Moscato Sabayon, nearly as rich as ice cream base, lends luxurious creaminess to this dense, decadent treat. Ole Smoky White Lightnin' Moonshine adds a faint boozy flavor to the cake and glaze, and, for me, fond memories of my grandfather sipping his "hooch" as he made barbecue on his homemade pit. Harried hosts take note: I think pound cake tastes even better the day after it's made, and the Moscato Sabayon sauce is easy to whip up an hour before you serve dessert.

MAKE THE CAKE: Preheat the oven to 325 degrees F. Grease and lightly flour a 10-inch Bundt pan.

Stir together the strawberries, ¼ cup sugar, and ¼ cup moonshine in a medium bowl; set aside.

In another medium bowl, sift together the flour, baking soda, baking powder, and salt; set aside.

In the bowl of a stand mixer or with a hand mixer, beat together the butter, remaining 2 cups sugar, and the vanilla and almond extracts on medium speed for 2 to 3 minutes, until the mixture is light and fluffy. Add the eggs, one at a time, and beat on low speed for 1 to 2 minutes, until well blended, scraping the bowl after each addition.

Add one-third of the dry ingredients to the butter and sugar mixture and beat on low speed until combined. Add half of the buttermilk and beat again, repeating the process until the remaining ingredients are added, ending with the dry ingredients and mixing until the batter is just combined. Do not over mix. Drain the strawberries and set the moonshine liquid aside for the glaze. Fold the strawberries and basil into the batter.

Pour the batter into the prepared Bundt pan and bake for 1 hour and 15 minutes, or until a toothpick inserted in the center comes out clean. Cool in the pan for 15 minutes, then remove the cake by inverting the Bundt pan over a wire rack and lifting it off the cake. Let the cake cool completely on the rack.

MAKE THE GLAZE: Puree the strawberries in a food processor until smooth.

In a saucepan, combine the pureed strawberries, 1 cup water, and the granulated sugar. Bring to a boil over medium-high heat, then reduce heat to low and simmer for 20 minutes, or until the mixture has a syrupy texture.

In a small bowl, make a slurry by stirring the cornstarch into 2 tablespoons cold water. Slowly whisk the slurry into the saucepan until the liquid thickens. Remove from the heat and pour the mixture through a fine-mesh strainer into a small bowl.

In a clean mixing bowl, combine the reserved moonshine mixture, strained strawberry liquid, and confectioners' sugar. Poke holes (I make a lot of holes) into the cake with a skewer or toothpicks, and drizzle or spoon all the glaze on the pound cake, on both top and sides. Set aside to allow the glaze to set.

MAKE THE SABAYON: Combine all the ingredients in a stainless steel bowl. Prepare an ice bath in a large bowl or fill your sink with ice and cold water.

Bring about 1 inch of water to a simmer in a large pot over medium heat. Set the mixing bowl on top of the pot of simmering water and whisk, being sure not to scramble the eggs, until the sugar is dissolved and the sabayon mixture thickens. Remove from the heat and sit the bowl in the ice bath for at least 20 minutes before serving. The texture should be like a loose pudding.

Serve slices of pound cake with spoonfuls of the sabayon. Leftover sabayon can be refrigerated in a covered container for 2 days.

CORNBREAD AND PECAN BREAD PUDDING *With Bourbon-Bacon Glaze*

SERVES 10 TO 12

8 cups cubed stale cornbread
   (recipe and instructions below)
3 cups chopped pecans, divided
1 teaspoon kosher salt
2 cups buttermilk
1 cup heavy cream
1 cups (2 sticks) unsalted butter,
   melted and cooled
1½ cup granulated sugar
1 teaspoon ground cinnamon
6 large eggs
4 teaspoons vanilla extract
1 cup packed light brown sugar
¼ cups all-purpose flour
4 tablespoons unsalted butter,
   at room temperature

BOURBON–BACON GLAZE
¾ cup buttermilk
½ cup (1 stick) unsalted butter
3 tablespoons light corn syrup
3 tablespoons bourbon
½ cup granulated sugar
½ cup packed light brown sugar
½ teaspoon ground cinnamon
1 teaspoon baking soda
1 teaspoon vanilla extract
3 slices bacon, cooked and
   crumbled

CORNBREAD
1½ cups fine cornmeal
1 cup all-purpose flour
½ cup granulated sugar
1 teaspoon salt
2 teaspoons baking powder
½ teaspoon baking soda
2 large eggs
1½ cups buttermilk
½ cup vegetable oil

Cornbread was a staple in my childhood home, as it was in many homes. My grandmother didn't bake much, but when she wanted something sweet, she would crumble cornbread into a bowl, sprinkle it with sugar, and pour buttermilk over the top. This recipe pays homage to those times I sat on her lap and shared this bowl of love with her. It's a combination of what Grandma called the Four Bs: Bacon, Bourbon, Buttermilk, and Bread.

The trick is to make the cornbread in advance, as stale cornbread works best for this pudding. I like to let it set out for 3 days so it becomes stale, dry, and hard—a perfect ending to a soulful supper.

Spray a 9 by 13-inch baking pan with nonstick baking spray.

In a large bowl, toss together the cubed cornbread, 2 cups pecans, and salt.

In a medium bowl, whisk together the buttermilk, heavy cream, melted butter, granulated sugar, cinnamon, eggs, and vanilla extract. Pour the wet mixture over the cornbread and pecans, and toss together gently with your hands. Transfer to the baking pan and set out at room temperature for 45 minutes so that the flavors soak into the cornbread.

Preheat the oven to 350 degrees F.

In a small bowl, stir together the brown sugar, flour, and room temperature butter with a fork until the mixture looks like crumbs. Mix in the remaining 1 cup pecans, then sprinkle the pecan topping evenly over the bread pudding. Bake for 35 to 45 minutes, until the pudding is slightly firm to the touch, and golden brown.

WHILE THE BREAD PUDDING IS IN THE OVEN, PREPARE THE GLAZE: In a medium saucepan over medium heat, mix together the buttermilk, butter, corn syrup, bourbon, granulated sugar, brown sugar, and cinnamon. Bring the

mixture just to a boil, then reduce the heat to low and simmer for 5 minutes, stirring often to prevent the syrup from burning. Whisk in the baking soda and vanilla. Off the heat, stir in the bacon crumbles, then let sit for 10 minutes before serving so that the glaze soaks up some of the salty, smoky flavor.

To serve, scoop servings of the bread pudding onto dessert plates (be sure you get those pecans) and drizzle with the glaze.

MAKE THE CORNBREAD: Preheat the oven to 400 degrees F. Grease an 8-inch-square baking pan with nonstick cooking spray.

In a large bowl, stir together the cornmeal, flour, sugar, salt, baking powder, and baking soda. Whisk in the eggs, buttermilk, and vegetable oil until well blended.

Pour the batter into the prepared pan and bake for 20 to 25 minutes, until a toothpick inserted in the center comes out clean. Let cool completely on a wire rack, then cut into 1-inch squares and leave out, uncovered, to dry for 3 days.

NAVY BEAN PIE

SERVES 8

1 (15.5-ounce) can navy beans,
  rinsed and drained
¾ cup evaporated milk
4 tablespoons unsalted butter,
  softened
2 large eggs
1¾ cups sugar
1 teaspoon ground cinnamon
½ teaspoon ground cardamom
½ teaspoon ground nutmeg
½ teaspoon ground ginger
1 teaspoon vanilla extract
1 teaspoon grated lemon zest,
  minced
1 tablespoon all-purpose flour,
  plus more for rolling the dough
1 recipe piecrust dough (page
  162), chilled

I was introduced to bean pies as a young girl during the Civil Rights movement. It was a staple in our neighborhood, introduced through members of the Nation of Islam—often sold by bow-tied men in neat suits, on street corners in urban communities. It is a humble dish with a strong legacy in African American cuisine, and a perfect example of how to make something wholesome and even wonderful out of the simplest ingredients. The mild and earthy flavor profile is very similar to sweet potato or pumpkin pie, and like those pies, it can be eaten warm or cold. I've never seen it used with any other bean, just navy beans.

Preheat the oven to 400 degrees F.

In a food processor, combine the beans and evaporated milk and process until smooth.

Using a hand mixer, cream together the butter, eggs, and sugar in a medium bowl until light and fluffy. Add the navy bean mixture to the bowl along with the cinnamon, cardamom, nutmeg, ginger, vanilla, lemon zest, and flour, and beat until well blended and smooth.

Remove the chilled piecrust dough from the refrigerator and let come to room temperature just long enough to roll out on a lightly floured surface. Using a floured rolling pin, roll the dough into a 12-inch circle approximately ⅛ inch thick. Roll the dough over the rolling pin, then gently roll it into the pie plate, pressing it gently into the dish. Trim excess dough away from the edges and crimp the edges with your fingers or a fork. Chill for 30 minutes.

Pour the filling into the chilled piecrust and bake for 10 minutes, then lower the heat to 325 degrees F and bake for another 40 to 45 minutes, until a toothpick inserted in the center comes out clean. Let the pie cool on a wire rack for 15 minutes before serving.

The pie can be made ahead and kept, covered with plastic wrap or foil, in the refrigerator for 1 week or frozen for up to 3 months.

LEMON BLUEBERRY BUCKLE

SERVES 8

STREUSEL TOPPING

½ cup all-purpose flour
½ cup granulated sugar
Pinch of salt
1 tablespoon grated lemon zest
4 tablespoons unsalted butter,
    cubed, at room temperature

BUCKLE

½ cup (1 stick) unsalted butter, at
    room temperature
1 cup granulated sugar
3 large eggs
1 tablespoon grated lemon zest
2 tablespoons fresh lemon juice
1¾ cups all-purpose flour
1 teaspoon baking powder
½ teaspoon baking soda
½ teaspoon salt
¾ cup vegetable oil
2 cups blueberries, fresh or frozen

WHIPPED CREAM

1 cup heavy cream, cold
¼ cup confectioners' sugar
2 teaspoons finely chopped
    fresh thyme
1 teaspoon grated lemon zest

I was first served a "buckle" when I was thirty years old, at a ladies' luncheon. I was quite confused as to what made it different from a "Betty," which I knew from my childhood. After some research, I found that while similar, the buckle's streusel topping causes it to buckle in the center, hence the name. The Betty has streusel throughout and doesn't buckle—which seems to be the main distinction—but I still don't know who Betty was. Both preparations work well with different seasonal fruits and both are simple and forgiving. The combination of lemon and blueberry is my go-to flavor pairing for spring and summer. This quick and easy dessert is perfect for warm days and barbecues.

MAKE THE STREUSEL: In a medium bowl, stir together the flour, granulated sugar, salt, and lemon zest. Using a fork, cut in the butter until the mixture is crumbly and resembles small peas. Cover the bowl and transfer to the freezer while you make the buckle.

MAKE THE BUCKLE: Preheat the oven to 350 degrees F. Generously spray a 9-inch-square baking pan with nonstick cooking spray.

In the bowl of a stand mixer or with a hand mixer, cream together the butter and granulated sugar for about 5 minutes on medium speed, until light and fluffy. Add the eggs, one at a time, scraping down the sides of the bowl after each addition. Add the lemon zest and juice.

In a medium bowl, mix the flour, baking soda, and salt.

Gradually stir one-third of the dry ingredients into the butter and sugar mixture until combined, then stir in one-third of the oil. Repeat the process in thirds until the remaining dry ingredients and oil are completely incorporated into the batter. Gently fold in half of the blueberries.

Pour the batter into the prepared pan and spread evenly with a spatula. Sprinkle the remaining blueberries over the top of the batter. Remove the crumb topping from the freezer and sprinkle it over the blueberries.

Bake for 40 to 45 minutes, until a toothpick inserted into the center comes out clean.

WHILE THE BUCKLE IS IN THE OVEN, PREPARE THE WHIPPED CREAM: Place a stainless steel mixing bowl in the refrigerator or freezer for at least 15 minutes, until very cold. Using a hand mixer, beat the cold heavy cream in the cold bowl at medium speed for about 90 seconds, until the cream thickens. Add the confectioners' sugar, thyme, and lemon zest, and continue to beat until the whipped cream holds a peak, about another 90 seconds. Cover the bowl and transfer to the refrigerator until ready to serve.

When the buckle is done, let cool on a wire rack for 30 minutes.

Serve the buckle with the whipped cream. Leftover buckle will keep for 2 to 3 days at room temperature.

RED VELVET CRÈME BRÛLÉE

With Vanilla Bean Cream Cheese Frosting

SERVES 6

8 large egg yolks, at room
  temperature
½ cup granulated sugar, plus
  more to caramelize the tops
1 teaspoon vanilla extract
¼ cup unsweetened dark cocoa
  powder, preferably Ghirardelli
1 cup heavy cream
1 cup buttermilk
⅛ teaspoon red food coloring

FROSTING
4 ounces cream cheese, softened
4 tablespoons unsalted butter,
  at room temperature
1 vanilla bean
½ cup confectioners' sugar
Sprigs of fresh mint (optional)

I am a red velvet fanatic and in this recipe I decided to blend two classics together, red velvet cake and crème brûlée. Choose a good-quality cocoa powder that will add deep chocolate flavor. To get the crème's texture just right, take your time when tempering the eggs—it will come out velvety smooth. Baking in a water bath insulates the ramekins from the heat of the oven, which also helps the crème's texture; the towel keeps them from sliding around in the water bath.

These can be made in advance and frozen for up to 3 weeks. To freeze, wrap each ramekin individually in plastic wrap after they come out of the oven and have cooled. The day before you plan to serve them, transfer from the freezer to the refrigerator overnight to thaw. When you're ready to serve, sprinkle sugar on top and caramelize it with a torch or place under the broiler for 2 to 3 minutes.

Set a clean kitchen towel in the bottom of a high-sided roasting or baking pan and arrange six 6-ounce ramekins (about 3½ inches in diameter) on the towel, leaving room between each. Bring 6 cups water to a simmer in a saucepan.

In a large bowl, whisk together the egg yolks, granulated sugar, and vanilla until well blended. Sift the cocoa over the egg mixture and whisk until smooth.

In another saucepan, warm the cream and buttermilk for 5 to 6 minutes over medium heat, until small bubbles just begin to form around the edge (steam will be rising from the cream). Very slowly, a little at a time, drizzle a small amount of the warm cream mixture into the yolk mixture, whisking continuously until the cream is fully incorporated— this is the tempering step; if you get scrambled eggs, start over and proceed more slowly. Add the red food coloring and whisk to combine.

Preheat the oven to 325 degrees F.

Strain the mixture through a fine-mesh sieve, then divide the custard among the ramekins. Carefully pour the hot water from the saucepan into the roasting pan, to come halfway up the sides of the ramekins; this creates the water bath.

Bake for 35 to 45 minutes, until the custard is set, but still jiggles slightly at the center.

Once the crème brûlées come out of the oven, remove them from the water bath and set them aside for 30 minutes to cool, then transfer them to the refrigerator and chill for at least 4 hours. At this point, you can wrap and freeze any of the not-yet-brûléed crèmes for later (see headnote).

While the ramekins chill, make the frosting: Combine the cream cheese and butter in a medium bowl and, using a hand mixer, beat until smooth and well blended. Split the vanilla bean and, using the back of a small knife, scrape the seeds out, discarding the pod. Add the vanilla seeds to the cream cheese and mix for 1 minute to combine. Sift in the confectioners' sugar and beat until smooth. Transfer to a medium piping bag, using a tip of your choice, and set aside.

About 30 minutes before serving, remove the ramekins from the refrigerator and let them come to room temperature.

Sprinkle a thin layer of granulated sugar over the tops of the crème brûlées. Caramelize the tops using a kitchen torch or place them under a hot broiler until the sugar is a deep golden-brown color and brittle to the touch.

Using a piping bag, squeeze a dollop of frosting on each crème brûlée. Serve with a fresh mint sprig as garnish, if you choose.

BENNE SEED WAFERS
With Chocolate Gravy

MAKES ABOUT 3 DOZEN WAFERS

WAFERS
1 cup benne seeds
1 cup packed brown sugar
4 tablespoons unsalted butter,
   at room temperature
1 large egg, beaten
1 teaspoon vanilla extract
1 teaspoon fresh lemon juice
½ cup all-purpose flour
¼ teaspoon kosher salt
¼ teaspoon baking powder

CHOCOLATE GRAVY
½ cup unsweetened dark cocoa
   powder, preferably Ghirardelli
4 tablespoons all-purpose flour
¾ cup granulated sugar
2 cups milk
3 tablespoons unsalted butter,
   softened
2 teaspoons vanilla extract
Pinch of salt

The benne seed was originally introduced to the United States through the slave trade of the 1700s. Benne seeds can be found easily online, but you can also substitute sesame seeds. Benne seeds have a rich, nutty flavor as compared to the lighter flavor of the sesame seeds. These delicious wafers have a very light, crisp texture, more like delicate tea cookies; wafers being lighter and thinner than sturdier cookies, which use more baking powder.

For a rich treat, I dip benne seed wafers in chocolate gravy. Chocolate gravy is a traditional Southern indulgence much loved from the Missouri Ozarks to the West Virginia Appalachians, usually served with fresh biscuits. This dessert is a great shared plate. The chocolate hardens only slightly at room temperature, and remains essentially a soft sauce; simply reheat to loosen back to pouring or dipping consistency.

MAKE THE WAFERS: Preheat the oven to 325 degrees F. Line a baking sheet with parchment paper.

In a small skillet over medium heat, toast the benne seeds for 8 to 10 minutes, until they're just turning brown, stirring often to prevent burning. Remove from the heat and let cool.

In a medium bowl, use a hand mixer to cream together the brown sugar and butter until smooth and creamy. Add the egg, vanilla, and lemon juice and mix until combined.

In a separate bowl, whisk together the flour, salt, and baking powder. Slowly add the dry ingredients to the brown sugar mixture and mix until the ingredients are fully incorporated and the dough is smooth. Stir in the benne seeds and refrigerate the dough, uncovered, for at least 30 minutes or up to 1 hour.

To bake the wafers, drop tablespoons of the chilled dough onto the prepared baking sheet, leaving 2 to 3 inches of space between each. Bake for 12 to 15 minutes, until the dough flattens into thin, crisp golden brown wafers. Set the baking sheet aside to cool for 5 minutes, then transfer the cookies to a wire rack.

MAKE THE CHOCOLATE GRAVY: Whisk together the cocoa, flour, granulated sugar, and milk in a medium saucepan until well incorporated. Set over medium heat and cook for 6 to 8 minutes, stirring continuously until the mixture thickens. Off the heat, whisk in the butter, vanilla, and salt.

To serve, pour the gravy into a soup bowl and arrange the benne seed cookies around the bowl. Dip the cookies into the chocolate and enjoy!

CHOCOLATE BUTTERMILK PIE

SERVES 8

PIECRUST

1¼ cups all-purpose flour, plus
  more for rolling
1 tablespoon sugar
1 teaspoon kosher salt
½ cup (1 stick) unsalted butter,
  cold, cut into cubes
⅓ to ½ cup buttermilk, cold

FILLING

4 large eggs
1½ cups sugar
½ cup (1 stick) unsalted butter,
  melted and cooled
¼ cup all-purpose flour
⅓ cup unsweetened dark
  cocoa powder, preferably
  Ghirardelli
½ teaspoon kosher salt
2 teaspoons vanilla extract
1 cup buttermilk

Whipped cream (page 154),
  for serving

Although this pie's roots are in the United Kingdom, it is considered a traditional pie of the South. My first introduction to buttermilk pie was in the home of Grandma Richey, my roommate's grandmother in Texas. She constantly overindulged us with good Southern meals that always included dessert. This pie was the perfect ending to Sunday supper. It's mildly sweet with deep chocolate flavor, smooth, and custardy, with a great tang from the buttermilk.

MAKE THE PIECRUST: Preheat the oven to 375 degrees F.

In a medium bowl, stir together the flour, sugar, and salt. Using a pastry cutter or a fork, cut the cold butter into the dry ingredients until the mixture resembles coarse crumbs. Make a well in the mixture and pour ⅓ cup buttermilk into the well. Using a fork, stir until the mixture is evenly moist. Add more of the buttermilk as needed to form a dough. Transfer the dough to a lightly floured surface and flatten into a thick round. Wrap in plastic wrap and refrigerate for at least 1 hour or up to 2 days.

Remove the chilled piecrust dough from the refrigerator and let come to room temperature just long enough to roll out on a lightly floured surface. Using a floured rolling pin, roll the dough into a 12-inch disc approximately ⅛ inch thick. Roll the dough over the rolling pin, then gently roll it into the pie plate, pressing it gently into the dish. Trim excess dough away from the edges and crimp the edges with your fingers or a fork. Chill for 30 minutes.

MAKE THE FILLING: In a large bowl, whisk together the eggs and sugar. Whisk in the butter, flour, cocoa powder, salt, vanilla, and buttermilk until smooth.

Pour the filling into the chilled piecrust and bake for 15 minutes, then reduce the heat to 350 degrees F and continue to bake for another 45 minutes, until a toothpick inserted in the center comes out clean.

Remove to a wire rack to cool completely. Slice and serve with whipped cream.

AUNT LUCILLE'S 7-UP POUND CAKE

SERVES 12 TO 16

1½ cups unsalted butter, at room temperature

3 cups granulated sugar

5 large eggs, at room temperature

1 teaspoon grated lemon zest

1 teaspoon lemon extract

1 teaspoons vanilla extract

3 cups cake flour, sifted

¾ cup 7-Up (see headnote)

7-UP GLAZE

1 cup confectioners' sugar

2 tablespoons fresh lemon juice

2 tablespoons 7-Up

1 teaspoon grated lime zest

In the Midwest, we drank pop—not soda, not Coke, but pop, the most popular being 7-Up. It was good for stomachaches, great with food, and was the star ingredient of the iconic 7-Up Cake. My Aunt Lucille would keep 7-Up by the case in her basement, reserved for herself and, sometimes, for me. Everyone else would get those no-name 10-cent sodas, and I would revel in the moments I was told to go down and fetch a couple of good pops exclusively for our enjoyment.

This is a pound cake, and the only cake I can ever remember my Aunt Lucille ever making. For me, it will always carry cherished memories of celebrations and good times. This is the kind of recipe that reminds you how good old-fashioned cakes were (and can be). If you don't already have a go-to pound-cake recipe, learn this one. Definitely use 7-Up for this recipe because it has a high level of carbonation that helps the cake to rise, and gives it a brighter, fresher lemon-lime flavor than other sodas.

The cake can be made well in advance, wrapped tightly in plastic, and frozen for up to 4 months. It will keep moist and can be pulled out to thaw several hours before serving. It's great served alone or with ice cream or fresh fruit compote.

Preheat the oven to 325 degrees F.

Spray a 10-inch Bundt or tube pan with nonstick cooking spray (see note).

In the bowl of a stand mixer or with a hand mixer, cream together the butter and granulated sugar for 5 to 7 minutes, until light and fluffy. Add the eggs, one at a time, scraping down the sides of the bowl after each addition. Add the lemon zest, lemon extract, and vanilla extract and mix until combined. Add the flour one-third at a time and mix on low speed, alternating with ¼-cup portions of the lemon-lime soda, mixing well after each addition.

Pour the batter into the prepared pan and bake for 1 hour to 1 hour 15 minutes, until a toothpick inserted in the center comes out clean. Let cool for 30 minutes, then invert onto a wire rack and lift the pan off of the cake. Let the cake cool on the rack.

While the cake cools, make the glaze: In a small bowl, stir together the confectioners' sugar, lemon juice, 7-Up, and lime zest until smooth.

Using a 6-inch wooden skewer or toothpick, poke holes in the top of the cooled cake. Slowly spoon the glaze over the cake, letting it run into the holes and over the surface. Set the cake aside for 10 minutes before serving to let the glaze absorb into the cake and give it a lightly lacquered finish.

NOTE: Don't skip this step unless you like digging your cake out of the pan! I swear by Baker's Joy Non-Stick Baking Spray with Flour and recommend a smoother Bundt pan for less chance of sticking.

BANANAS FOSTER BANANA PUDDING

SERVES 12

6 large egg yolks
2 cups evaporated milk
½ cup half-and-half
1½ cups granulated sugar
¼ cup all-purpose flour
¼ teaspoon kosher salt
1 teaspoon vanilla extract
½ cup (1 stick) unsalted butter
½ cup packed light brown sugar
¾ teaspoon ground cinnamon
¼ teaspoon ground cloves
8 ripe bananas, peeled and
  sliced
½ cup dark rum
2 (8.8-ounce) packages Biscoff
  cookies (35 to 40 cookies)
2 cups heavy cream, very cold
1 teaspoon confectioners' sugar

Banana pudding is a must-have dessert on any soulful table. It is a classic comfort dish that can be served to any age group, at any event—everyday dinners, church meetings, and always, always as part of a holiday spread. Bananas Foster was created at Brennan's Restaurant in New Orleans as a fancy dessert for fancy diners. I figured if I put the two together, I would come up with a dessert that could balance haute with humility, along the lines of an English trifle with a punch to it. For richer, toastier vanilla flavor, I've ditched the traditional 'nilla wafers and use Biscoff cookies in their place. (If you love vanilla wafers, by all means go ahead and use those, just keep in mind they have a more crumbly texture.) This pudding can be made the day before, chilled, and removed from the refrigerator when it is time to serve. Be sure to use ripe bananas for this dish; if necessary, let them sit for several days till bright yellow with some small brown spots.

If you've never flambéed or torched a dessert, there's no need to panic. Make sure you use long matches, stand back, and have confidence that the flame will subside in seconds. Take all proper precautions with open flame, such as making sure you're in a well-ventilated space and have a fire extinguisher handy. You don't want to skip this step, because the process of caramelizing the bananas delivers the flavor of the rum without the actual alcohol, and really makes the dessert special.

I like to use a footed trifle bowl for a dramatic presentation, but you can serve the banana pudding in individual glasses or a 9 by 13-inch baking dish. The pudding needs to chill for at least 6 hours or overnight before serving, so this is a great make-ahead dessert for entertaining.

In a large bowl, whisk together the egg yolks, milk, and half-and-half until combined.

In another bowl, stir together the granulated sugar, flour, and salt.

With a wooden spoon or spatula, stir the dry ingredients into the milk mixture until combined. Transfer to a large saucepan and set over medium heat. Cook, stirring constantly, for 10 minutes, or until the mixture thickens. Stir in the vanilla and remove the pan from the heat. Off the heat, strain the pastry cream through a fine-mesh sieve and set aside.

In a large skillet, melt the butter over medium heat. Stir in the brown sugar, cinnamon, and cloves, and cook for 5 to 7 minutes, until the mixture begins to bubble and the sugar has melted. Add the sliced bananas and gently stir for 3 to 5 minutes, until the bananas begin

to caramelize. Add the rum but do not stir. Using a long match, very carefully light the contents of the skillet and stand back. When the fire dissipates, stir the bananas in the sauce (it will happen quickly as the alcohol in the rum burns away), then set the pan aside to cool.

In a trifle bowl or serving dish, form a base layer of Biscoff cookies (break them as needed to fit). Top with one-third of the banana mixture, then one-third of the pastry cream. Repeat two more times for a total of 3 layers. Cover with plastic wrap and chill for 6 hours or overnight.

Just before serving, whip the cream until foamy, add the confectioners' sugar, and continue to beat until the cream holds stiff peaks. Using a spatula or a piping bag, top the banana pudding with the whipped cream. Serve immediately.

Necessities

Sweet Tea Barbecue Sauce

Duck-Fat Grits Croutons

Compound Butters

Buttermilk Dressing

Buttermilk Gravy

White Lightnin' Butter Sauce

Green Tomato Chimichurri

Dark Cherry Gravy

Kumquat Marmalade

Pickled Mustard Seeds

Apple-Cranberry Mostarda

Tomato-Persillade Hot Sauce

Vanilla Bean Remoulade

Roasted Garlic and Caramelized
Onion Jam

Pickled Green Stems

Bourbon Peach Jam

Smoked Tomato Relish

Black-Eyed Pea and Collard Green Spoon Bread

Avocado Hoecakes

SWEET TEA BARBECUE SAUCE

MAKES ABOUT 2 CUPS

1 cup ketchup
½ cup strong brewed ice tea, well sweetened
¼ cup apple cider vinegar
¼ cup packed brown sugar
2 tablespoons Worcestershire sauce
1 teaspoon kosher salt
1 teaspoon onion powder
1 teaspoon garlic powder
1 teaspoon ground cumin
1 teaspoon chili powder
1 teaspoon fresh lemon juice
½ teaspoon cayenne pepper
1 tablespoon Dijon mustard
2 teaspoons liquid smoke

This is a Kansas City–style sticky, sweet barbecue sauce with a spicy punch. The addition of tea gives a nice balance to the sweet and the heat, and adds a hint of something delightfully different that you can't quite put your finger on. A perfect sauce to enhance ribs (page 38), it can be used on any cut of grilled pork, beef, chicken, or even vegetables.

In a saucepan over medium heat, whisk all the ingredients together and simmer for 10 minutes to blend the flavors. Remove from the heat and set aside to cool.

Store in an airtight container in the refrigerator for up to 3 weeks or freeze for up to 6 months.

DUCK FAT GRITS CROUTONS

MAKES ABOUT 50 CROUTONS

1 cup milk
2 tablespoons unsalted butter
1 cup quick-cooking grits
2 teaspoons kosher salt
¾ cup grated Parmesan cheese
2 large eggs, beaten
6 ounces duck fat (about ½ cup)

Duck fat and grits! How soulful can you get? These little flavor bombs will add savory pop and crunch to anything you add them to—salads, soups, or stews. Duck fat is available from specialty markets or butchers and can be found online.

In a saucepan, combine 2 cups water, the milk, and butter and bring to a boil over medium-high heat. Slowly whisk in the grits and return to a boil, whisking continuously. Reduce the heat to low and stir in the salt and Parmesan. Cook for 20 to 25 minutes, stirring often, until the grits have softened. Set the pan aside to cool for 10 minutes, stirring occasionally.

Once the grits have cooled, whisk in the eggs until incorporated, moving quickly in order to temper the yolks and not get scrambled eggs.

Grease an 8-inch-square baking pan with nonstick cooking spray. Pour in the grits mixture, smoothing the top with a spatula. Transfer to the refrigerator and chill, uncovered, for at least 2 hours, or until firm.

Once the grits mixture has firmed up, turn it out from the baking pan onto a work surface and cut into 1-inch squares. (If you aren't using it all at this time, return the unused portion to the pan, cover with plastic wrap, and refrigerate for up to 5 days.) Transfer the cut squares to a plate. Line a second plate with paper towels for draining.

In a medium nonstick skillet, melt enough duck fat to cover the bottom of the pan and bring to 325 degrees F over medium heat. Add the cut croutons to the hot fat in batches, being careful not to crowd the pan, and cook for 1 to 2 minutes per side, until nicely browned and crisp. Transfer to the paper-towel-lined plate to drain and repeat with the remaining croutons.

COMPOUND BUTTERS

Compound butters are a quick, easy way to enhance the flavor of many dishes, from warm bread or rolls and simple steamed vegetables to roasted chicken or steaks straight off the grill. The simple technique always reminds me of Br'er Rabbit's old-school mixture, molasses whipped together with oleo (margarine), to serve with hot biscuits straight from the oven. The following are some of my favorite and most used blends, both sweet and savory.

These compound butters can be refrigerated, tightly covered, for 5 to 7 days or frozen for up to 6 months. I just store them in a plastic container with a cover and spoon out what I need, but if you want to present them at the table, store these butters in crocks or ramekins.

CINNAMON, GINGER, AND STAR ANISE BUTTER

This sweet and spicy butter is great with waffles, French toast, corn-bread, or biscuits.

MAKES 1 POUND

1 cup (2 sticks) unsalted butter, cold
1 whole star anise
2 teaspoons peeled and chopped fresh ginger
1 cinnamon stick
1 cup (2 sticks) unsalted butter, at room temperature
½ teaspoon ground cinnamon
¼ teaspoon ground ginger

In a small saucepan over very low heat, melt the cold butter, then add the star anise, ginger, and cinnamon stick and let cook for 15 minutes to infuse the flavors into the butter. The butter may brown slightly, but be careful not to let it burn. Remove from the heat and set aside to cool for 5 minutes. Strain the infused butter through a fine-mesh sieve into a bowl, discarding the whole spices and solids.

In a food processor or in a mixing bowl with a wooden spoon, whip the room-temperature butter until smooth. Add the ground cinnamon and giner and mix on low speed to incorporate. Continue mixing while you slowly drizzle the infused butter into the bowl and blend the two together until uniform in color.

Transfer the butter into airtight, lidded containers and store in the refrigerator or freeze.

CITRUS MOLASSES BUTTER

Try this blend with green vegetables, such as asparagus, Brussels sprouts, or broccoli.

MAKES 1 POUND

1 tablespoon grated lemon zest
1 tablespoon fresh lemon juice
1 tablespoon grated orange zest
1 tablespoon fresh orange juice
2 tablespoons molasses
1 pound (4 sticks) unsalted butter, at room temperature

In a small bowl, combine all the ingredients and mix with a wooden spoon or hand mixer until smooth. Transfer the butter into airtight, lidded containers and store in the refrigerator or freeze.

LEMON, CRACKED BLACK PEPPER, GARLIC, AND BASIL BUTTER

This combination goes as well with fish and seafood as on chicken and steaks. Use the coarsest setting on your grinder or mill to fully appreciate the pepper's flavor and heat.

MAKES 1 POUND

2 tablespoons grated lemon zest
2 tablespoons fresh lemon juice
4 cloves garlic, minced
2 tablespoons freshly cracked black pepper
½ cup finely chopped fresh basil
1 pound (4 sticks) unsalted butter, at room temperature

In a small bowl, combine all the ingredients and mix with a wooden spoon or hand mixer until smooth. Transfer the butter into airtight, lidded containers and store in the refrigerator or freeze.

BUTTERMILK DRESSING

MAKES ABOUT 4 CUPS

1½ cups mayonnaise
½ cup sour cream
2 cups buttermilk
1 teaspoon kosher salt
1 teaspoon granulated garlic
1 teaspoon granulated onion
1 teaspoon cracked black
  pepper
1 tablespoon chopped flat-leaf
  parsley
1 teaspoon chopped fresh
  oregano
1 teaspoon chopped fresh thyme
1 tablespoon chopped fresh
  chives

This dressing is so universally loved, it doesn't need an explanation. The extra herbs just add a notch to the flavor factor. It's not only great for salads, you can use it atop salmon, fried green tomatoes, or as a dip for chicken wings.

In a food processor, combine the mayonnaise, sour cream, buttermilk, salt, granulated garlic, granulated onion, and pepper and process until smooth. Pulse in the fresh parsley, oregano, thyme, and chives until just combined. The dressing should be creamy but with a pleasing texture from the herbs.

Transfer to an airtight container and chill for at least 1 hour before serving. The dressing will keep in an airtight container in the refrigerator for 7 to 10 days.

BUTTERMILK GRAVY

MAKES ABOUT 3 CUPS

4 tablespoons unsalted butter

1 shallot, minced

¼ cup all-purpose flour

2 cups vegetable broth

1 cup buttermilk

2 tablespoons chopped fresh
thyme

1 teaspoon chopped fresh
sage

1 teaspoon chopped fresh
rosemary

1 tablespoon cracked black
pepper

2 teaspoons kosher salt

Traditional buttermilk gravy was developed in the Appalachian South. It is commonly made with sausage drippings, and is sometimes referred to as sawmill gravy. The high fat content of the buttermilk adds flavor, and the addition of sage and thyme mimic the flavor of sausage. This recipe contains no meat, so it's a good option for vegetarian friends. It works very well as a sauce over most vegetables, as well as for biscuits or toast. If you prefer the more familiar version, you can brown and add some crumbled sausage.

In a medium saucepan, melt the butter over medium-high heat. Stir in the shallot and sauté for about 2 minutes, until starting to soften. Whisk in the flour to coat the shallot and make a roux. Cook for about 2 more minutes, whisking continually, until the roux turns a medium golden brown (as a rule, the darker the roux the deeper the flavor of the sauce, but we're going for something lighter here).

Whisk in the vegetable broth until the gravy begins to thicken, then reduce the heat to low and slowly pour in the buttermilk. Continue to simmer for 5 minutes, then add the chopped sage and rosemary, pepper, and salt. Cook for about 15 more minutes to blend the flavors and until the gravy is your desired thickness.

Serve over Fried Green Tomatoes (page 101) or your favorite vegetables. The gravy will keep in an airtight container in the refrigerator for up to 1 week.

WHITE LIGHTNIN' BUTTER SAUCE

MAKES ABOUT 2 CUPS

½ cup champagne vinegar

¼ cup dry white wine

⅓ cup White Lightnin' Moonshine

1 teaspoon fresh lemon juice

3 tablespoons finely minced
  shallots

1 teaspoon kosher salt, plus
  more as needed

½ teaspoon Old Bay Seasoning

¼ teaspoon ground white pepper

1 cup (2 sticks) unsalted butter,
  chilled and cut into 10 pieces

3 tablespoons finely chopped
  flat-leaf parsley

3 tablespoons finely chopped
  fresh tarragon

3 tablespoons finely chopped
  fresh chives

Freshly ground black pepper

Traditional beurre blanc is an emulsified butter sauce that's great with fish or seafood. This down-home version of the classic calls for the addition of moonshine, specifically Ole Smoky White Lightnin' Moonshine (which can be purchased legally, thank you). The taste profile is a cross between vodka and whiskey, and adds a sharpness and hint of heat that marries well with the richness of butter, creating an unexpectedly refined flavor. Try this sauce on the Pumpkin Seed–Crusted Trout (page 128) or Crab Loaf (page 143).

In a medium saucepan, combine the vinegar, wine, moonshine, lemon juice, shallots, salt, Old Bay, and white pepper over medium heat. Bring the mixture up to a low boil, then reduce the heat to medium-low and simmer for 20 to 25 minutes, until the liquid has reduced to ¼ cup.

Reduce the heat to low. Rapidly whisk in 2 pieces of cold butter a time into the reduction until only 2 pieces are left.

Remove the saucepan from the burner and whisk in the remaining butter off the heat until the sauce is smooth and creamy. Whisk in the parsley, tarragon, and chives and season with salt and black pepper. Serve immediately.

GREEN TOMATO CHIMICHURRI

MAKES ABOUT 2½ CUPS

1 to ½ cups coarsely chopped
 green tomato (about 1 large)
6 cloves garlic, smashed
½ cup chopped cilantro
½ cup chopped flat-leaf parsley
¼ cup chopped fresh oregano
 leaves
¼ cup red wine vinegar
¾ cup extra-virgin olive oil
2 teaspoons kosher salt
½ teaspoon red pepper flakes

Many cultures have created a green sauce of some sort to complement their cuisine, including pesto, persillade, pistou, hilba, chowchow, and chimichurri, to name a few. And I love them all! In Argentina, I was first introduced to chimichurri served with a beautiful piece of Argentinian beef. In this recipe, I combined the beloved Southern chowchow with the traditional Latin sauce. It has since become my go-to sauce for grilled meats and poultry. It touches on an array of flavors: the tartness of the tomato, the fragrant freshness of herbs, acid from the vinegar, and heat from the pepper flakes. The combination is a little tart, a little tangy, and a little pungent—it adds great flavor to anything it touches, but especially a perfectly grilled steak (page 45)!

In a food processor, combine the chopped tomato, garlic, cilantro, parsley, and oregano. Pulse a few times until the mixture is finely chopped.

Pour into a medium bowl and whisk in the vinegar, olive oil, salt, and red pepper flakes.

Transfer to an airtight container and chill for at least 2 hours. Store in the refrigerator for 2 to 3 weeks or freeze for up to 3 months. Bring to room temperature before serving.

ᗪARK CHERRY ᗱRAVY

MAKES ABOUT 3 CUPS

3 tablespoons unsalted butter
1 shallot, chopped
¼ cup coarsely chopped onion
¼ cup coarsely chopped celery
¼ cup coarsely chopped carrot
¼ cup all-purpose flour
5 cups low-sodium beef broth,
   at room temperature, divided
1 bay leaf
10 to 12 whole black peppercorns
2 cups frozen dark cherries (12
   to 14 ounces), thawed
¼ cup balsamic vinegar
1 teaspoon kosher salt
1 teaspoon cracked black pepper

This recipe is a cross between gravy and barbecue sauce, so I serve it with smoked meats, pork, and poultry. The result is actually a lot richer in flavor than your average gravy because the technique is similar to that of a French demi-glace, but a lot less complicated. Try it especially on the Cocoa-Crusted Rack of Lamb (page 36)— the cherry adds a nice fruity note that plays against the slightly bitter char from the cocoa on the lamb.

In a medium saucepan, melt the butter over medium heat. Stir in the shallot, onions, celery, and carrots and cook for 5 minutes, or until the onions are translucent. Sprinkle in the flour and cook, stirring, for 3 minutes, or until the mixture starts to brown. Whisk in 4 cups beef broth, increase the heat to medium-high, and bring just to a boil. Immediately reduce the heat to low, add the bay leaf and peppercorns, and simmer for about 40 minutes, until the liquid has reduced by half. Remove from the heat and strain the gravy through a fine-mesh strainer, discarding the solids.

Return the gravy to the saucepan over low heat and stir in the remaining 1 cup of beef broth, the thawed cherries, and balsamic vinegar. Simmer for 15 minutes, then season with the salt and pepper.

Store in the refrigerator for 3 to 5 days or freeze for up to 2 months. Reheat over low heat before serving.

KUMQUAT MARMALADE

MAKES ABOUT 3 CUPS

8 to 10 ounces kumquats
  (about 1½ cups)
1 teaspoon grated lemon zest
1 tablespoon fresh lemon juice
1 teaspoon peeled and minced
  fresh ginger
4 cups sugar
1 cup fresh orange juice

This tangy recipe is slightly looser in texture than some jams, because I don't add pectin beyond that found naturally in the kumquat seeds. It falls somewhere between honey and preserves in density, with all the tangy flavor and brilliant orange color of a classic marmalade.

Cut the kumquats in half and remove the seeds. Place the seeds in a layered square of cheesecloth and tie the ends together with kitchen twine to make a small sachet. Clean the white pith from the kumquats by gently scraping it out with a paring knife, then slice the kumquat rind into slivers.

In a large pot, combine the slivered kumquat rind, sachet of seeds, lemon zest, lemon juice, ginger, sugar, orange juice, and 5 cups water. Cover and let sit for 4 hours at room temperature.

Uncover the pot, place over medium heat, and cook the kumquat mixture for 15 minutes, stirring often to prevent sticking. The sugar will dissolve and the mixture will thicken slightly. Then reduce the heat to low and simmer for about 1 hour, until the mixture is very thick.

Carefully extract the seed sachet from the hot mixture and set it aside to cool before handling. Once cool, using your hands, squeeze the sachet over the mixture to return any pectin from the juices to the marmalade (being careful not to tear the bag and drop the seeds). Continue to cook the marmalade over low heat for another 18 to 20 minutes, until it gels. The marmalade will be slightly thicker than honey. Turn off the heat and let the pot cool to room temperature.

Transfer the marmalade to airtight containers and keep in the refrigerator for up to 3 weeks.

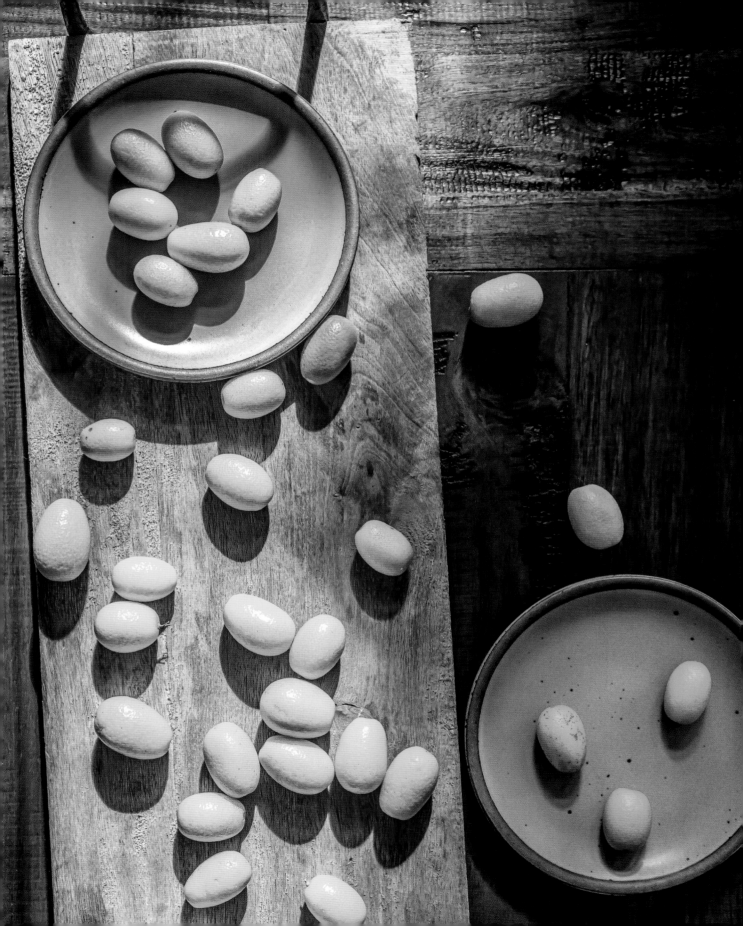

PICKLED MUSTARD SEEDS

MAKES ABOUT 1 CUP

½ cup whole yellow mustard
  seeds
¾ cup champagne vinegar
1 teaspoon kosher salt
1 bay leaf
1 teaspoon ground turmeric
1 tablespoon honey, or to taste
¼ teaspoon red pepper flakes
1 clove garlic, unpeeled

With this condiment, you'll look at mustard in a whole new way. Its intense flavors combine with a texture that pops in your mouth, adding a fun, bold heat to any roasted or smoked meat, charcuterie or rich cheese, or fried fish. I love this as a substitute for jarred mustard and consider it to be a perfect topping for Bologna Mousse (page 28) or with Blue Cornmeal–Crusted Fried Fish (page 140).

I prefer champagne vinegar because its smooth flavor best complements the mustard seeds without overpowering them, but you could use any white wine vinegar.

Rinse the mustard seeds in a fine-mesh sieve, then transfer them to a small bowl.

In a small saucepan, combine the champagne vinegar, salt, bay leaf, turmeric, honey, red pepper flakes, and garlic with ½ cup water and set over medium heat. Bring just to a boil, then add the mustard seeds. Reduce the heat to low and simmer for 20 minutes, or until the mustard seeds plump slightly and the mixture thickens. Remove from the heat and set the saucepan aside to cool.

Once cool, transfer the pickled mustard seeds to an airtight container and chill at for least 4 hours before serving. The pickled mustard seeds can be kept in an airtight container in the refrigerator for up to 6 weeks.

APPLE-CRANBERRY MOSTARDA

MAKES ABOUT 3 CUPS

2 cups peeled, cored, and
   coarsely chopped Granny
   Smith apples
¼ cup fresh lemon juice
1 cup fresh or frozen, thawed
   cranberries
¼ cup champagne vinegar
½ cup port
1 cup sugar, divided
1 cinnamon stick
2 sprigs fresh thyme
¼ cup minced shallots
1 tablespoon grated orange zest
¼ cup yellow mustard seeds
1 teaspoon kosher salt
⅛ teaspoon ground cayenne
   pepper

As in many places, fall in Georgia is synonymous with delicious apples, so I make it a seasonal tradition to include some type of apple dish on my Thanksgiving table. It's a direct play on the sweet-savory condiment of Italy, with my soulful-girl touch and a bit of Americana. It's an unexpected, tangy option to serve alongside or in place of a traditional cranberry sauce. Try it with Candied Duck Wings (page 58), or with just about any pork roast, chop, or tenderloin.

Toss the chopped apples in the lemon juice (to prevent browning) and set aside.

In a medium saucepan, combine the cranberries, vinegar, port, ½ cup sugar, and the cinnamon stick with 2 cups water. Bring the mixture just to a boil over medium-high heat, then reduce the heat to low and simmer for 20 minutes, stirring occasionally. Stir in the apples, thyme, shallot, orange zest, mustard seeds, remaining ½ cup sugar, salt, and cayenne pepper. Simmer over low heat for another 15 minutes, or until the apples are softened and the flavors meld. Remove the cinnamon stick and let cool.

The mostarda will keep in an airtight container in the refrigerator for up to 2 weeks. Bring to room temperature before serving.

TOMATO-PERSILLADE HOT SAUCE

MAKES 1½ CUPS

¾ cup flat-leaf parsley leaves

1 large red tomato, coarsely
chopped

6 cloves garlic, unpeeled

2 jalapeños, seeded and
diced

½ cup extra-virgin olive oil

2 tablespoons fresh lemon
juice

2 tablespoons white vinegar

1 tablespoon kosher salt

Persillade is a green sauce widely used in French cuisine, especially Provençal cooking. Because I love condiments, I decided to make a flavorful hot sauce with this recipe. I use both tomato and jalapeños to achieve that. You can even use this as a salsa with chips if you like. It has a smooth, heavy texture, unlike the chunky store-bought hot sauce, and more depth of flavor.

Combine all the ingredients in a food processor and puree until smooth and well blended. Transfer to an airtight container and refrigerate until ready to use. Serve at room temperature. The hot sauce can be kept in an airtight container in the refrigerator for 1 week.

VANILLA BEAN REMOULADE

MAKES ABOUT 1¾ CUPS

1 cup mayonnaise
2 whole vanilla beans, split
  lengthwise and seeds scraped
¼ cup ketchup
¼ cup sweet pickle relish
¼ teaspoon chopped flat-leaf
  parsley or tarragon
1 teaspoon fresh lemon juice, or
  to taste
Pinch of kosher salt

This is hands-down the best remoulade for seafood I've found and also the easiest: The sweetness of the vanilla and herbal-anise kick from the tarragon both beautifully complement the natural flavors of crab, lobster, or any rich fish. Simply stir it together and chill until ready to serve. Use it with the Lobster Beignets (page 121), Crab Loaf (page 143), or simple steamed shellfish for a luxurious starter.

In a small bowl, combine the mayonnaise and vanilla seeds. Let sit at room temperature for 5 minutes, then stir in the ketchup, relish, parsley, and lemon juice. Finish with a pinch of salt and chill until ready to serve. The remoulade keeps in an airtight container in the refrigerator for up to 2 weeks.

ROASTED GARLIC AND CARAMELIZED ONION JAM

MAKES ABOUT 1½ CUPS

4 heads of garlic, outer papery
  skins removed
2 tablespoons extra-virgin olive
  oil
3 tablespoons unsalted butter
2 medium yellow onions, cut in
  half and thinly sliced
½ cup packed brown sugar
¼ cup balsamic vinegar
1 teaspoon kosher salt
½ teaspoon freshly cracked
  black pepper

Garlic and onion are essential ingredients to so many cuisines. Although they enhance dishes throughout the world, they rarely get to be the star of the show. This recipe changes all that! In London, at the famous Harrods Food Hall, I fell in love with an outstanding onion, garlic, vinegar, sugar, and salt concoction served with their greens and meat. I recreated it with this recipe, and I guarantee it's a tasty addition to the Shrimp and Crab Fritters (page 120), as well as any pork or beef dish or cheese plate.

Preheat the oven to 375 degrees F.

Carefully trim ¼ inch from the top of each garlic bulb and the same amount from the bases to expose the cloves on both sides. In a bowl, rub the olive oil over the garlic to thoroughly coat. Wrap the bulbs tightly in aluminum foil, set on a baking sheet, and roast for 45 minutes. The garlic is done when it is soft to the touch and smells amazing. Remove from the oven and let cool in the foil at room temperature for 15 minutes.

When cool, remove the garlic from the foil and squeeze out the individual cloves into a small bowl. Discard the skins and husks.

In a medium saucepan, melt the butter over medium heat. Add the onions, stir to coat them with the butter, and cook for 12 to 15 minutes, stirring occasionally. Add the roasted garlic to the pan along with the brown sugar, ½ cup water, the balsamic vinegar, salt, and pepper. Stir well to combine, reduce the heat to low, and cook for 30 minutes, stirring every 10 minutes and occasionally scraping the bits up from the bottom of the pan to incorporate them into the jam, until the onions are brown and the jam is thick. Remove the saucepan from the heat and set aside to cool for 30 minutes.

Transfer the jam to an airtight container and store in the refrigerator for up to 10 days. When you are ready to use, warm the jam in the microwave for 30 seconds.

PICKLED GREEN STEMS

MAKES 2 PINTS

2 cups stems from leafy greens
(see headnote)
1½ cups white vinegar
1 tablespoon kosher salt
2 cloves garlic, smashed
1 jalapeño, seeded and sliced
1 bay leaf, crushed
1 tablespoon whole black
peppercorns
1 tablespoon whole yellow
mustard seeds
2 tablespoons chopped mixed
fresh herbs, such as a
combination of thyme, basil,
and cilantro

If you eat leafy greens, this is a perfect way to utilize the whole plant by pickling the stems. Any hardy green stems works well—kale, chard, collards, turnip greens, or mustard greens are all perfect for this quick-pickling method.

Cut the stems into 1- to 2-inch lengths and divide them between two clean pint jars with lids.

In a large saucepan, bring all the remaining ingredients plus 1 cup water just to a boil over medium-high heat. Remove the pan from the stovetop and carefully pour or ladle the hot brine into the jars, but do not put the lids on yet.

Let the stems steep uncovered until the brine has completely cooled. Once cool, screw on the lids, transfer to the refrigerator, and chill for at least 48 hours before serving. The pickled stems will keep in the refrigerator for up to 2 weeks.

BOURBON PEACH JAM

MAKES ABOUT 2 CUPS

3 cups peeled and chopped
   fresh peaches (6 to 8 large
   peaches, or 1½ pounds)
½ cup peeled and grated
   Granny Smith apple
½ cup granulated sugar
1 cup packed light brown sugar
2 tablespoons fresh lemon juice
1 teaspoon ground ginger
1 teaspoon vanilla extract
2 cinnamon sticks
¼ cup bourbon

Put these two ingredients together and it's magic, any way you do it. What else can I say? This jam is a natural for buttered toast or biscuits, but I love to use it on the Duck Schnitzel and Sweet Potato Waffles (page 74).

This recipe calls for a quick-canning process, but it's good to boil the jars just to make sure they are sterile. Plus, I find that putting the hot jam into hot jars tempers it better than using cold jars.

Place 2 small plates in the freezer; these will be used to test the jam later.

In a large saucepan, bring the chopped peaches, granulated sugar, brown sugar, lemon juice, ginger, vanilla, and cinnamon sticks just to a boil over medium-high heat, stirring occasionally. Reduce the heat to low and cook, uncovered, for 40 to 50 minutes, stirring often, until the mixture thickens. Remove from the heat and stir in the bourbon. Let sit for 15 minutes to allow the flavors to meld.

To test whether the jam has set, remove a plate from the freezer. Spoon about 1 teaspoon of jam into the center of the plate then return it to the freezer for 2 minutes. Remove the plate and drag your finger through the jam—it should leave a trail across the plate. If it doesn't and the jam is still too runny, return the pot to low heat and cook for another

5 minutes, then repeat the test on the second chilled plate. Once the desired consistency is reached, skim any foam off the top of the jam.

While the jam cools, bring a large pot of water to a boil over medium-high heat. Very gently lower two 8-ounce mason jars plus their lids and rings into the pot for 5 minutes to sterilize the jars. Carefully remove the jars, lids, and rings from the water and let dry.

When the jars are just cool enough to handle (but still hot), ladle the hot jam into the jars, then let them cool, uncovered, to room temperature. Screw on the lids and rings, transfer to the refrigerator, and chill for at least 16 to 24 hours, until the jam sets. The jam can be kept in an airtight container in the refrigerator for up to 2 months.

SMOKED TOMATO RELISH

MAKES ABOUT 2 CUPS

20 whole Roma tomatoes (3 to 4 pounds)
1 cup diced green bell pepper
1 cup diced red bell pepper
1½ cups diced yellow onion
¾ cup extra-virgin olive oil
2 jalapeños, seeded and diced
3 cloves garlic, minced
⅓ cup red wine vinegar
2 tablespoons finely chopped fresh mint
2 tablespoons finely chopped cilantro
2 tablespoons sugar
1 tablespoon kosher salt
1 tablespoon cracked black pepper

The surprising flavor of this relish is somewhat like a barbecue sauce and I love to use it on a vegetarian dish, where its smoky fragrance and umami flavors trigger satisfying food memories of meat cooked over coals. Use this relish on the Collard Green Caesar (page 110) or on grilled or roasted vegetables, fish, and even pork.

Soak 1 chunk of hickory wood in water for 30 minutes.

Prepare a charcoal grill for low, indirect heat by removing the grate and arranging a small mound of charcoal on one side of the grill. Ignite the coals and once they turn white, place the soaked wood atop the charcoal, spray the grate with nonstick cooking spray, and replace it on top of the grill.

Place the tomatoes directly on the grate on the cool side of the grill (not over the coals), cover, leaving the vent slightly open, and smoke for 30 minutes, turning when necessary to prevent burning. Set aside to cool.

Chop the cooled smoked tomatoes and, in a large bowl, toss them with all the remaining ingredients to combine. Let sit for 10 minutes before serving to allow the flavors to meld. The relish can be kept in an airtight container in the refrigerator for up to 2 weeks.

BLACK-EYED PEA AND COLLARD GREEN SPOON BREAD

SERVES 12

¼ cup extra-virgin olive oil
½ cup diced red bell pepper
½ cup diced onion
3 tablespoons minced garlic
(about 9 cloves)
3 cups fine- or medium-grind
yellow cornmeal, sifted
2 quarts milk
½ cup unsalted butter, melted
1 teaspoon kosher salt
2 teaspoons Lawry's Seasoned
Salt
1 tablespoon garlic powder
1 tablespoon onion powder
12 large eggs, beaten
3 tablespoons baking powder
2 cups cooked collard greens,
drained and seasoned (page 86)
1 (15.8-ounce) can black-eyed
peas, drained

Spoon bread is an old-school dish that has been around for years. It's similar to British Yorkshire pudding and Native American Indian pudding, but more like a baked dressing. I've experimented with many different combinations, but black-eyed peas and collard greens just makes sense when you consider that both reach their fullest potential when eaten with a slice of cornbread. If you like basic spoon bread, this recipe definitely takes the flavors up a notch. As a side, it goes well with pork or fowl. Leftovers can be frozen in a covered container for up to 1 month.

Preheat the oven to 350 degrees F.

Generously grease a 13 x 9-inch baking pan.

In a large saucepan, heat the olive oil over medium-high, and sauté the red pepper, onion, and garlic for 3 to 5 minutes, until the onion is translucent. Reduce the heat to medium, stir in the cornmeal and 1 quart milk, and cook for about 5 minutes, stirring frequently, until smooth. Add the remaining 1 quart milk and cook for another 10 to 12 minutes, continuing to stir, until the mixture thickens. Stir in the melted butter, salt, seasoned salt, garlic powder, and onion powder.

Remove the pan from the heat and slowly fold in the beaten eggs, baking powder, greens, and black-eyed peas. Transfer the batter into the prepared baking pan and bake for 35 to 45 minutes, until the top is golden brown and a toothpick inserted into the center comes out clean.

AVOCADO HOECAKES

MAKES ABOUT THIRTY 4- TO 5-INCH HOECAKES

1 medium ripe avocado
  (about 6 ounces)
2 cups self-rising cornmeal
1 cup buttermilk
¼ cup finely diced red onion
¼ cup vegetable oil, plus
  additional oil for frying
¼ cup finely diced red bell
  pepper
1 tablespoon chopped cilantro
  leaves
2 large eggs
1 jalapeño, finely diced

A hoecake falls somewhere between a pancake and cornbread. These cakes were a common fare of slaves—the story is that they were actually cooked on field hoes, or a griddle that resembled a hoe shape, held over a fire. I'm not certain of their origins, but they have been around in my family as far back as I can remember. Plain hoecakes were served to me as one of my first baby foods, mashed up with pot liquor from the collard greens.

Hoecakes are an easy quick bread adaptable to many variations, both savory and sweet. In this recipe, they are savory with a hint of spice. The avocado, onion, and peppers give moisture, flavor, and texture. These are great served warm or at room temperature, and leftovers can easily be reheated in a low oven. Try them in place of biscuits during the summer with any of the compound butters on page 172, or with Oxtail Rillettes (page 14).

Peel and pit the avocado. In a food processor or blender, puree the avocado until smooth and creamy, about 1 minute.

Scrape the processed avocado into a medium bowl and add the cornmeal, buttermilk, onion, vegetable oil, red pepper, cilantro, eggs, and jalapeño. Mix until the batter is well blended and thick; it should not be runny.

Add just enough oil to a large skillet or griddle to coat the bottom, and heat over medium-high until shimmering. Drop about 2 tablespoons batter into the skillet for each hoecake and cook for about 2 minutes, until browned and crisp, then flip and cook on the other side for about 2 more minutes, until browned. Repeat until all the remaining batter is used. Leftover batter will keep in the refrigerator for up to 3 days.

INDEX

(Page references in *italics* refer to illustrations.)

ACKNOWLEDGMENTS

This book represents a longtime dream that has been realized. First I would like to thank my family, my community, and the many people I have met throughout my life journey who have shared your hearts, your food, and your recipes. From the dinner tables I have sat at, to the conversations on the flight attendant jump seats, where we shared our love of food through stories, each interaction has been meaningful in helping to develop the recipes and ideas in this book.

To Janice Shay, for keeping me from going insane, supporting, and believing in me, I could not have done this without you. You have truly become my partner in crime. We are no longer just colleagues—we are true friends. I thank you, your husband, and Punch.

Jono Jarrett, you get me! And that says a lot. You truly became a vessel that transported my soul onto these pages. Getting to know you and sharing my vision through food and words has been a huge highlight for me. You taught me the importance of my own voice and helped me to understand why it deserved such a big space in this world. I felt protected through your guidance and appreciate you for seeing something special in me and for welcoming me into the Rizzoli family.

Noah Fecks, the camera was genius in your hands. Your quick eye for detail is unmatched. I am humbled by the effort and enthusiasm that comes across in each photo. You did more than take pictures, you created my world for all to see. Your photography captured the depths of the memories I explore through food, and I am honored to have worked with you.

Thanks also to Sydney Wallace, Deandre Kitchen, Calvin Moses, Joana Duffie, Tiffanie Barriere, Jim Farmer, Annette Joseph, Justin Williams, Barbara Pederzini, John & Jennifer O'Connell, Larissa Dubose, Drez Ryan, Amber Martinez, Victoria Granoff, Mars, Bennie, and Bella.

To my mother and father in heaven. There's not a day that goes by that I don't thank God for blessing me with the two of you to shape and mold me. I wish you were alive to see and rejoice in my accomplishments. In spite of your earthly absence, I feel your pride shining down upon me. You both taught me how to make art with the most modest of ingredients. Your guidance allowed me to travel far and always embrace the love in food and celebration. This book will serve as a memory of all that you wanted for me.

My wife, Lorraine, and my daughter, Kursten, you two are my backbone. Your support, your love, your faith are my lifeline. You have kept me grounded and provided everything I needed to make this project come to life. Your cheers have been louder than a sporting arena, and your arms are always out to catch me and push me back up when I think I'm about to fall. It took several years, but WE did it!

Years of globetrotting culinary adventures have given Chef **Deborah VanTrece** a good idea of what people of many cultures consider comfort food. Following a brief career as a flight attendant, she graduated as valedictorian of her class at the Art Institute of Atlanta. Working as Executive Chef for a catering company, she enjoyed great success during the 1996 Summer Olympics in Atlanta cooking for events for international athletes, dignitaries, and visitors. With her wife, VanTrece opened the acclaimed Twisted Soul Cookhouse and Pours in 2014 and since then its award-winning soul food has appeared on numerous "Best of" lists, with features in the *The New York Times*, the *Atlanta Journal-Constitution*, *Eater Atlanta, Thrillist, Buzzfeed, Kitchn, Southern Kitchen*, and *Food & Wine*. The author's unique voice, professional accomplishments, and personal story have generated interest in her featured talks on the NYT Cooking channel on You-Tube; Cherry Bombe Radio; on NPR; appearances on scores of podcasts; and recently the James Beard Foundation Boot Camp for Policy and Change. This is her first cookbook.

"Chef Deborah VanTrece has taken her brilliantly colorful imaginative culinary passion for global nuances and bold flavors to heart in this beautiful, exciting, eatable bible of soulful recipes. A must have celebration of life, food and love . . . on a plate!"
— ALEXANDER SMALLS, James Beard Award-winning chef, author, and restaurateur

"Deborah VanTrece has spent her entire cooking career as a scholar of all things soul food across the globe. The Twisted Soul Cookbook is the gift of a lifetime of lessons from generations of traditions in nourishment and celebrations. I can not wait to cook my way through this book with the ingenious flair of Deborah's perspective and personality." — KELLY FIELDS, chef and author of The Good Book of Southern Baking

"The recipes in The Twisted Soul Cookbook make my mouth water. Chef Deborah VanTrece brings her vibrant personality and eclectic background to the dishes she has created here. I can't wait to taste them." — TANYA HOLLAND, award-winning chef, restaurateur, and author of Brown Sugar Kitchen

"Reading through Deborah VanTrece's recipes is like taking a walk down memory lane of my childhood in the South. Fresh salmon croquettes are warmly familiar, a mustard greens take on Caesar salad is a brilliant twist, and a sweet tea barbecue sauce is an inspired idea I wish I had thought of first. It's a collection of recipes with universal appeal—whether you live in the South or not—but stamped with Deborah's singular point of view."   — BEN MIMS, cooking columnist for The Los Angeles Times